# FARES ABRAHAM

# NEXTGEN
# **LEADERS**

---

## LEARNING TODAY HOW TO
## CHANGE TOMORROW

FOREWARD BY CHIP INGRAM

Published by Levant Media.
Washington DC USA.
levantministries.org

International Standard Book Number: 978-0-692-92763-2
Printed in the United States of America.

Unless otherwise indicated, Scripture is taken from the Holy Bible, New Living Translation, copyright © 1996 by Tyndale House Foundation. Used by permission of Tyndale House Publishers, Inc., Carol Stream, Illinois 60188. All rights reserved.

While the author has made every effort to provide accurate Internet addresses at the time of publication, neither the publisher no the author assumes any responsibility for errors or for changes that occur after publication.

Graphic Design by Cristina Bullon.
Photo Credit: Gloria Estrada.

I dedicate this book to my awesome
wife, Soha, whose steadfast support
keeps me going and serving, and to
my crazy precious twins, Josiah and
Annalie, my own next generation.

# CONTENTS

# FOREWARD

will never forget the first time I met Fares Abraham. Our missions pastor had built a relationship with Fares in the Middle East and was eager for me to meet him.

He told me about this young man's heart, his love for next generation leaders, his huge steps of faith, and the impact that he was having here in the United States and around the world.

"Chip, you've got to meet him. I think you two will really connect and he's someone we're very interested in getting behind."

It was one of those seasons in my life where I was completely overwhelmed with deadlines, travel and responsibilities. I didn't have an hour to spare, and yet more than once I was urged to give Fares a little time.

Against my already establish priorities, I agreed to spend exactly one hour with him.

Fares walked into my office and began to share his story and his heart. I tried to keep emotionally neutral, fulfill my one-hour commitment and move on with the rest of my day. But God had a better plan that was far different than mine... I looked up at the clock and three hours had zoomed by and neither of us could stop talking!

Something happened that I didn't expect. I caught his heart and passion and became acutely aware that the Holy Spirit was going to use this man's life in a very significant way. I went from "I don't have time" to "I have to MAKE the time to help this man fulfill the vision that God has placed on his heart."

Since then, Fares and I have partnered together in ministry to equip and disciple emerging leaders through the combined work of Levant Ministries and Living on the Edge. I've had the privilege of speaking at several NEXTGEN conferences, and Fares has often spoken boldly from the pulpit of Venture Christian Church.

What you hold in your hands is more than one man's journey. *NEXTGEN Leaders* is a playbook, or manual, to move you from a "want to be leader" to a "leader of influence" for this generation.

It's biblical, practical, well-researched and filled with the kind of inspiring passion that must be caught, not taught. It's what I experienced in my office when God brought Fares Abraham into my life.

Now, I invite you to give him the time that I gave him. It will take less than three hours to go through this book, but it will take a lifetime for the principles and truth of this book to get through you.

The world is in desperate need of godly, faith-filled leaders. Everything rises and falls with leadership—it is our only hope for the next generation. I encourage you... Be One Of Those Leaders!

Chip Ingram

Senior Pastor, Venture Christian Church

President & Teaching Pastor, Living on the Edge

# INTRODUCTION

Leadership is not about the next election.
It's about the next generation.

— Simon Sinek —
author and motivational speaker[1]

I was born and raised in Jesus' backyard, in the little town of Bethlehem (Matt. 2:1). Yet Christ remained a stranger to me throughout my entire youth. I didn't know the gospel. I didn't know I could be delivered from my sins. And I certainly didn't know I could escape the sorrow that filled my soul, sorrow born of my experiences growing up in the Holy Land.

My family didn't have a lot of money, nor was it easy for me to get an education. And, of course, there was the unending violence. I can still so vividly remember, when I was just ten years old, seeing my mother shot by a soldier for no reason at all. Fortunately, she lived. But my friend, Salam, was not so lucky. When he was only fourteen, this young boy was shot in the head, in his own home, while his mother was cooking dinner. I was angry. I was scared. I was confused. To be honest, I didn't know what direction I'd go. But God had a plan for me all along. As Jeremiah says, "'I know the plans I have for you,' says the Lord. 'They are plans for good and not for disaster, to give you a future and a hope'" (Jer. 29:11).

My incredible journey to the Lord started on the day my father took a leap of faith by placing his trust in me. I can still recall, like it was yesterday, the moment he pulled me aside, saying, "Son, I haven't even received my high school diploma. But I want you to pursue a better and brighter future. You go to the United States." That was an uncertain moment for me. But once I got to America in 1998, I realized my father knew what he was doing. In the United States I found a kind of freedom I'd never known. I was given opportunities I couldn't believe. And, most importantly, I heard the good news of Jesus Christ.

## ". . . SWEET LAND OF LIBERTY"

Life in America, at first, wasn't easy. I literally had nothing and I could barely speak English. Fortunately, the Alyateem family hosted me from day one, until I could get on my feet. They embraced me, sheltered me, fed me, and encouraged me. I don't know what I would have done without them. And I'll be eternally grateful for all of their love and support.

Eventually, I went to Liberty University, where I heard Pastor Rick Warren (Saddleback Church) speaking at a conference on finding God's purpose. He talked about many things, but what affected me the most was his teaching on how we're not here by accident. "God has a purpose for each of us," he explained. "It's based on how He created us." As Rick says in *The Purpose-Driven Life*: "The purpose of your life is far greater than your own personal fulfillment, your peace of mind, or even your happiness. It's far greater than your family, your career, or even your wildest dreams and ambitions. If you want to know why you were placed on this planet, you must begin with God. You were born *by* his purpose and *for* his purpose."[2]

This was a radical thought to me—i.e., that God had made me for some reason(s) that went far beyond just getting an education, achieving a successful career, or making money. Suddenly, as I let this truth sink into my soul, God started transforming how I perceived not only my own life, but life around me. I started seeing the "big picture." I realized God had implanted in me specific gifts so I could be successful. I don't mean "successful" in any selfish way for my own benefit. I mean "successful" in a way that would enable me to reach others for Christ.

So, I went to my spiritual mentor, Pastor Jadd Boulos, and told him: "I want to be baptized into God's family. I want to declare Jesus as my Lord and Savior. I want to commit myself to ministry."

That's when God really grabbed my life, saying, *Just as I've transformed so many others, I'm going to transform you. Despite your background, regardless of where you've come from, no matter what you've done, I'll always love you. I'll support you. I'll use you.*

I responded by surrendering to His promises, praying, "Lord, may your will be done in my life."

## GOD'S PURPOSE IN ME

Today, as I look back over the years since that special day when I gave 100% of my life to the Lord, I can see a steady line of godly helpers, especially Pastor Jadd. He was a true man of God, a real hero of the faith, a great husband, awesome father, and amazing prayer warrior. Both he and his wife, Jane, gave me incredible support. Pastor Jadd taught me, discipled me, and showed me God's ways. And unlike many so-called "Christian" leaders these days, his words actually matched his deeds. He talked the talk and walked the walk. He was always there for me, not only encouraging me to keep moving forward with God, but also advising and supporting me when I shared with him the burden that God had placed on my heart for my unsaved brothers and sisters in the Middle East.

I'll never forget what Pastor Jadd said when I told him my dream for a ministry to Arabic-speaking people. He said, "Fares, you lead, I'll follow. You must increase and I must decrease. And we both must decrease and He must increase."

"No way," I answered. "You are like my father. I look up to you."

"You don't get it," he replied.

"Then, please, help me understand."

"I jump," Pastor Jadd said, his voice full of wisdom. "You tell me how high."

I slowly began to understand. Pastor Jadd, being a humble servant who only wanted to honor God, was passing his baton of leadership to me—lovingly, gently, joyfully, and humbly.

Not long afterward, on one of the most painful days of my life, I had to visit Pastor Jadd on his deathbed. There, as he lay dying of Stage IV cancer, I said, "Pastor, I need you. You can't go now. You are the only one I can serve with."

But he responded, "There are more than 7,000 men better than me. Ask God to open your eyes to see them. And He will."

Pastor Jadd was right. Since his passing, God has shown me the men and women who have been there all along, fellow believers who, like me, are dedicated to serving God and committed to ministry. And together we've made a difference for Christ and for His Church around the world. But more needs to be done. More workers need to be found, called, trained and sent throughout Earth's field of lost souls. "'The harvest is great, but the workers are few,'" Jesus said. "'So pray to the Lord who is in charge of the harvest; ask him to send more workers into his fields'" (Luke 10:2). This is more true today than ever before in the history of the Church. Countless potential workers for the Kingdom of God are waiting to be gathered up and prepared for ministry. They visit our churches every weekend. They work in our communities every day. They live in our homes. They are known as today's Millennials—our next generation of leaders. They are . . . *you.*

## YOU ARE THE NEXT GENERATION

Life is not about us. It's about God. It's about His work *in* us and *through* us. Scripture puts it this way: "[W]e are God's masterpiece. He has created us anew in Christ Jesus, so we can do the good things he planned for us long ago" (Eph. 2:10). In other words, our Lord can take the smallest desire to do His work and turn that desire into spiritual and supernatural power, the kind of power we need to accomplish *His* will, in *His* way, throughout *His* world.

This is the simple purpose of Levant Ministries (the non-profit ministry I started in 2013): *share the good news of Jesus with the hopeless and helpless.* This is also the reason I wrote the book you hold in your hand, which I pray will be used as a tool to equip, train, and empower NextGen church leaders. But why does it matter? Why do the NextGen leaders of tomorrow need to be equipped, trained, and empowered today? Because I believe it's a biblical mandate.

We're commanded to prepare the way for those coming after us so that the faith "entrusted once for all time to his holy people" (Jude 3) will be preserved and passed on to others. Look at the relationship between Timothy and Paul. Timothy, unlike Paul, was not only a young person, but new in ministry. He had a lot of learning, growing, and changing to do. He also had troubling health issues, struggled with fear, and more than anything else, he was inexperienced. This is why Paul told the Corinthians that when Timothy arrived in Corinth, they should make sure he was at peace, not afraid or intimidated (1 Cor. 16:10).

Timothy may have even been a bit shy about sharing his faith, which we can assume from Paul's words: "[N]ever be ashamed to tell others about our Lord. And don't be ashamed of me, either, even though I'm in prison for him. With the strength God gives you, be ready to suffer with me for the sake of the Good News" (2 Tim. 1:8). Paul encouraged Timothy, saying, "You have heard me teach things that have been confirmed by many reliable witnesses. Now teach these truths to other trustworthy people who will be able to pass them on to others" (2 Tim. 2:2). Paul saw Timothy's shortcomings. Yet he still wanted to equip, train, and empower him. And Timothy ultimately did the same thing for others.

And so, I'm reaching out to all of you who are reading this book, to tell you that you'll be the ones to lead the Church in the days ahead. In fact, as members of the next generation, you'll likely expand the Kingdom of God faster than any other previous generation because of the modern tools of communication and technology you'll have at your disposal. You, therefore, represent not only the continuity of the gospel, but the continuity of the Church.

*NEXTGEN Leaders* is designed to shine a spotlight on these very important issues so that you, as part of the next generation of leaders, can begin preparing yourself *today* in order to change the world *tomorrow*. "Let this be recorded for future generations, so that a people not yet born will praise the Lord" (Ps. 102:18).

---
1
---

# FIND THE RIGHT
# CHURCH FOR YOU

There's something about the church that unites people in a way nothing else can. The church is a place where we ought to celebrate diversity as a reflection of the kaleidoscopic personality of God. Too often it's not, but when it is it's a beautiful thing because it unites people that would otherwise be divided.

— Mark Batterson —
National Community Church[3]

I traveled to America for reasons that had nothing to do with God. Having come from an entrepreneurial family, my objective was to succeed in a similar field. I wanted to earn a degree, start my own business, and become wealthy. I longed for a future better than the one I would have found in the Middle East. So, once I arrived in the United States, I began pursuing my goal with gusto. I definitely wasn't a Christian. At the same time, however, I enjoyed being with a small group of Arabic-speaking believers in Charlotte, North Carolina, where I'd settled.

I saw genuine love among these men and women. And I gained comfort by going to their Bible studies on Fridays and their church services on Sundays, even though they weren't very high-tech—no flashy lights, no expensive cameras, no big-screen TVs, no impressive orchestra. It was a simple church. In fact, there often weren't even musicians for the worship service! Everyone just sang as best they could out of a songbook. But we had each other . . . and God.

Eventually, after I'd finally met Jesus at college and committed my life to Him, I returned to my little Arabic church family in Charlotte, where I wanted to be baptized. I called the pastor and excitedly said, "Your messages now make sense to me! All that you've been saying about God makes sense now! I want to be baptized. I want to be part of the Church, and part of this church." The time had come for me to join a church, rather than just watch one from the sidelines. I needed to grow, change, serve, and live 100% for God. And that small church, at that time in my life, was the right church for me. It was a new beginning.

After graduating from college, I moved to Washington DC, where I attended the first Arabic-speaking evangelical church in North America. I was the Assistant Pastor and on the Board of Directors, under the leadership of Pastor Esper Ajaj, who loved and encouraged me to serve passionately. I later joined Church of the Redeemer, my current church, where I founded Levant Ministries. My ministry was born out of a meeting I had with senior pastor, Dale O'Shields. A true miracle of like-mindedness occurred as I began sharing with him my dream and vision. I soon discovered that he, too, felt a God-given passion for people of the Middle East. Then, after I received my church's full support, I started Levant Ministries. This marked another new chapter in my life.

Through my experience, I learned a valuable lesson: *we shouldn't despise our humble beginnings.* It doesn't matter whether you're in a small church or a big church, God works in both. The Lord saved me at a small church, then used me at a big church. Perhaps God has done the same thing in your life. Or, maybe He saved you at a large church and is now using you at a small church. Either way, it doesn't matter. The most important thing is that you be connected to others in the place God wants you to be. Believe me, when you get linked-in with like-minded people, great things start to happen. But it all must begin with finding the right church *for you*.

## UNDERSTAND CHURCH

What is "church"? A building? A gathering of people in a specific place at a predetermined time? A social club that meets regularly? A place where you can always hear a great sermon and enjoy amazing music? According to the Bible, none of these things are "church." In fact, we haven't even asked the right questions. We must actually ask two altogether different, but similar sounding, questions: 1) What is *the* Church?; and 2) What is *a* church?

First, *the* "Church" refers to people (Acts 8:3). The term is translated from the New Testament word *ekklesia*, which means "called out" (Acts 11:26; 1 Cor. 15:9). Jesus himself used *ekklesia* (or an Aramaic equivalent), when he declared, "'[Y]ou are Peter (which means 'rock'), and upon this rock I will build my church [*ekklesia*], and all the powers of hell will not conquer it'" (Matt. 16:18). It refers to persons whom God has "called out" of darkness (Eph. 5:8–13) and into His wonderful light (1 Peter 2:9). We, who are the *ekklesia*, were also "called out" of:

- a sinful lifestyle (1 Cor. 6:11; Eph. 4:22), into a mode of behavior/speech that is pure/holy (Eph. 4:29; 1 Thess. 4:7; 1 Peter 1:15–16; James 2:10);

- a mindset based on worldliness (James 4:4), into a way of thinking that is rooted in godly attitudes, ideas, priorities, and truths (Rom. 12:2; Phil. 4:8–9; Col. 3:2; 1 John 2:15–17);

- a state of estrangement from our Creator (Rom. 5:10; Col. 1:21), into God's family of redeemed children (John 1:12–13; Rom. 8:15).

Second, *a* "church" refers to the actual gathering of God's people in a community. This use of the term also comes from *ekklesia*, which can alternately be translated as "assembly" or "congregation," depending on its context (Acts 7:38). Interestingly, the word *ekklesia* was not widely used as a religious term throughout the Greek culture of the New Testament era. It was a *political* term signifying a group of citizens assembled to deliberate government issues. This may give us a hint of the biblical concept involving God's people on earth being citizens of heaven (Eph. 2:19; Phil. 3:20), in subjection to, and under the authority of, King Jesus (Rev. 19:16).

## ETHNIC OR MULTI-CULTURAL?

At this point it's crucial to mention a side issue that's caused some debate— churches formed to serve the needs of only one ethnic/racial population: e.g., Korean, Arab, Black, or Hispanic/Latino. The reasoning behind this "homogeneous unit principle" is that a church will grow faster "when the gospel is propagated along existing social lines and networks and when people do not have to cross ethnic, cultural, or class barriers to become Christians."[4] Such thinking is sometimes even extended beyond ethnic/racial bounds, going so far as to group people "into churches demarcated by ethno-linguistic distinctions, tribal or caste distinctions, social and economic status, education level, profession, and even common affinity groups—such as churches for cowboys or NASCAR-lovers (this is not hyperbole, Google them!)"[5]

It's understandable why Christians would enjoy worshiping alongside others with whom they share a common background, language, or experience. But this setup isn't the model presented in scripture. The earliest churches planted beyond Jerusalem were multi-racial/multi-ethnic. Consider the events that took place on the day of Pentecost, when the Holy Spirit energized and filled every believer with power from on high. Gathered together at this event were "Parthians, Medes, Elamites, people from Mesopotamia, Judea, Cappadocia, Pontus, the province of Asia, Phrygia, Pamphylia, Egypt, and the areas of Libya around Cyrene, visitors from Rome (both Jews and converts to Judaism), Cretans, and Arabs" (Acts 2:5–11).

We also see a multi-racial/multi-ethnic community in Antioch, where Christ's followers were first called "Christians" (Acts 11:19–26, 13:1–33). This church included Jews, Africans, Greeks, and Syrians. Unity in the midst of diversity was also taught by Paul, who said "you are all one in Christ Jesus" (Gal. 3:28). In 1 Corinthians 12:13, he explained, "Some of us are Jews, some are Gentiles, some are slaves, and some are free. But we have all been baptized into one body by one Spirit, and we all share the same Spirit."

Our need for unity is of paramount importance, as my good friend John S. Dickerson—nationally-awarded American journalist and author—has pointed out in his important volume, *The Great Evangelical Recession*. According to Dickerson, many evangelicals seem to have forgotten that unity among Christians is meant to be a validation of Christ's identity as the Messiah sent by the Father (John 17:23). "[U]nity is a guaranteed apologetic for His followers," explains Dickerson. "Because Jesus took this seriously, we'd better start taking it seriously."[6]

Obviously, first century churches were based on total unity of all those who came to Christ, which naturally created a multi-racial/multi-ethnic system. Yet this God-ordained model of corporate fellowship exemplified by Christ's earliest followers isn't being replicated by many American congregations. As of 2013, a Lifeway Research survey of over 1,000 Protestant pastors, 994 churchgoers, and 1,000 Americans showed that 86% of congregations were "predominantly one racial or ethnic group."[7] Yet more than half of the churchgoers (53%) said they *disagreed* with the statement: "My church needs to become more ethnically diverse."[8] Ed Stetzer, executive director of LifeWay, found these results troubling. "[M]ost people are happy where they are—and with whom they are," he observes. "Yet, it's hard for Christians to say they are united in Christ when they are congregating separately."[9]

But things are beginning to slowly change. According to Mark DeYmaz— founding pastor of Mosaic Church and author of *Building a Healthy Multi-ethnic Church*—a growing number of churches "are now describing themselves as 'multi-ethnic,' 'multiracial,' or 'multicultural' on their websites, and conferences are including sessions devoted to multi-ethnic ministry."[10] This is a good thing, says DeYmaz, who has correctly noted that "nowhere in the New Testament will you find the apostle Paul or anyone else encouraging us to plant or develop churches focused on specific people groups!"[11]

One of the reasons I attend my church is because of its multi-cultural, multi-ethnic, multi-racial quality. Such a quality is consistent with the biblical model of church. And none of us should abandon that model in favor of the emotional/social comfort obtained through involvement with a church based on: a) national origin; b) common language; or c) racial/ethnic identity. Local churches, generally speaking, should foreshadow that great day prophesied by John: "I saw a vast crowd, too great to count, *from every nation and tribe and people and language*, standing in front of the throne and before the Lamb. They were clothed in white robes and held palm branches in their hands. And they were shouting with a great roar, 'Salvation comes from our God who sits on the throne and from the Lamb!'" (Rev. 7:9–10).

## RECOGNIZE A GOOD CHURCH; IDENTIFY A BAD CHURCH

There are many good churches and wonderful ministries throughout the world, but we don't need to be involved with all of them. In fact, our only responsibility is to make a commitment to one church community in which we can serve God. It's within this context that God will further direct us toward any other places he may want us to work for the Kingdom.

It's like getting married. There are many wonderful people in the world who possess admirable qualities, lead inspiring lives, and have great personalities. But we don't marry all of them. We explore our options (e.g., get to know others, share experiences with others, compare our feelings when we're with others). Ultimately, we choose one person to whom we want to give ourselves, one life to merge with our life. This doesn't mean the unchosen were unworthy, ungodly, or unlovable. It just means that the person we picked was a better match to the individual we were created to be. They were a better fit to the life we were called to live.

Keeping with the marriage analogy, it should also be noted that people often hold wrong perceptions. Some people think marriage is all about securing perfect happiness. Others want to get the most attractive mate. And many feel they need to be married before a certain age. But there's far more involved in choosing a spouse. It's about: 1) finding who will best enable you to do what God wants you to do; 2) discovering who will help you become the person God wants you to be; and 3) identifying the man/woman with whom you'll best glorify God. I, for example, have been blessed beyond my wildest dreams through my amazing wife, Soha. Because I married her, I've gone much further in fulfilling my mission than I would have gone without her.

Having the right spouse will always enable you to aim higher, grow stronger, go farther, and achieve greater results. The wrong spouse, however, will always slow you down and perhaps even cause you to miss God-ordained opportunities. This is why choosing a mate is one of the most important decisions anyone will ever make. It's crucial that you carefully take your time to find the right spouse. The wrong spouse could hinder your emotional, intellectual, and spiritual progress. They might create unnecessary sufferings and trials. The wrong spouse could even temporarily delay God's plans for you. Similarly, it's vital for you to find the right church. Landing in a wrong church could be disastrous, or at least, result in major setbacks. So, if you're serious about doing anything for God, then you must get plugged into a vibrant, spiritually-minded, Jesus-following, biblically-centered church of like-minded believers (Heb. 10:25).

Bill Hybels—creator of Global Leadership Summit and founder/senior pastor of Willow Creek Community Church—has inspiringly expressed the importance of this biblical principle by describing the church's glorious nature, which sets it apart from every other organization:

> Its beauty is indescribable. Its power is breathtaking. Its potential is unlimited. It comforts the grieving and heals the broken in the context of community. It builds bridges to seekers and offers truth to the confused. It provides resources for those in need and opens its arms to the forgotten, the downtrodden, the disillusioned. It breaks the chains of addictions, frees the oppressed, and offers belonging to the marginalized of this world. Whatever the capacity for human suffering, the church has a greater capacity for healing and wholeness.[12]

Unfortunately, a lot of people, especially millennials, harbor a deep aversion to church involvement. This aversion may exist for several reasons, the most destructive one being a flawed idea of church gleaned from some not-so-reliable sources: magazines, pop culture, TV, avowed enemies of Christianity (e.g., atheists, humanists), and tragic stories told by individuals who have endured terrible church experiences. These sources corrupt our view of church, making us vulnerable to either: a) disillusionment when a church doesn't meet our unrealistic expectations; or b) negative biases that keep us from even starting to explore our church options. Both problems have hindered many people needing a church in which to mature (2 Peter 3:18).

## DETECT WARNING SIGNS

There are warning signs, of course, of a bad church. These might include a prideful body of leaders (Is. 42:8); an over-emphasis on money/finances (1 Tim. 6:10); a tolerance of sinful behavior (1 Cor. 5:1–13); doctrinal aberrations (1 Tim. 4:16; 2 Tim. 4:3); or unbiblical philosophies (e.g., the *number* of members is more important than the *quality* of members, or it's more important to grow *programs* than it is to grow *people*). If such issues are present, then it might be best to look elsewhere. But worship music, dress (casual vs. formal), or the stressing of one ministry over another (e.g., evangelism vs. social action) aren't disqualifying factors.

Oddly, sometimes the best way to evaluate a church is not by contemplating what church *should* be, but by thinking about what church *shouldn't* be. An enlightening list of what a church *shouldn't* be appeared in "What is Church?" by Mark D. Roberts, former Senior Pastor of Irvine Presbyterian Church in Southern California (1991–2007) and Executive Director of the Max De Pree Center for Leadership at Fuller Seminary. According to Roberts, a Harvard graduate, who has taught at Fuller Seminary and San Francisco Seminary, church is *not* (or shouldn't be): a *concert*; a *school*; a *club*; a *store*; or a *hospital.* Mistakenly thinking that "church" is indeed like any of these kinds of organizations will invariably lead to confusion, disappointment, and spiritual immaturity.[13] In other words, church doesn't exist to merely: provide great music; fill our heads with knowledge; make us feel like we're part of a group; inspire temporary loyalty (like a new fashion/fad); or treat us like patients who never become caretakers ourselves. We attend a church to glorify/praise/worship God, grow spiritually, and serve/support others.

## THE BOTTOM LINE

So, if a church is not a concert, school, club, store, or hospital, then what is it?

First, a church should be *a reflection of "the" Church*, which is described in scripture as the Body of Christ (1 Cor. 12:27). It's defined in Ephesians 1:23 as "his body; it is made full and complete by Christ, who fills all things everywhere with himself." This is an extraordinary remark that's been interpreted multiple ways to highlight different nuances of thought, but in essence it's saying that "the church is the 'completion or filling up' of his power and glory" and that Christ's "dominion would not be complete without the control over his church, and that is so glorious, that it 'fills up' the honor of the universal dominion, and makes his empire complete."[14] Also present here is a clear reference to Christ's deity and sovereignty, as renowned scholar Albert Barnes has noted: "[T]he passage teaches not only his supremacy, but demonstrates his universal agency, and his omnipresence—things that pertain only to God.[15]

Second, a church should be a *place of grace*. What is grace? The most basic definition is "unearned favor." It describes the means by which God reached out to save undeserving sinners (Titus 2:11–12). A biblically-sound, healthy, and Christ-glorifying church will *always* be grace-oriented, rather than law-oriented. Why? Because "God saved you by his grace when you believed" (Eph. 2:8–9; Rom. 5:20). Moreover, just as we've been shown grace by God through His forgiveness, patience, love, kindness, gentleness, and understanding, we ourselves must show grace toward others—believers *and* unbelievers. In a *place of grace* there's a balance between not judging (Matt. 7:1–3) and lovingly speaking the truth (Eph. 4:15). There are at least nine marks of a grace-oriented church, says Dr. Charles Bing, founder/director of GraceLife Ministries, who has also served as a pastor for nearly twenty years:

1. Grace is taught and preached consistently. . . . Assurance of salvation is available to all who believe in the promises of God. Likewise, our subsequent Christian growth is based on grace just as our initial salvation was.

2. People are encouraged to grow in grace. Grace gives people both motivation to grow and room to make mistakes while it gently guides them into maturity. . . . A church that is serious about making disciples will help people grow deep in the Christian life.

3. Grace is the primary motivation for Christian living. . . . Preaching and teaching does not make people feel unnecessarily guilty. Instead of emphasizing what we are or are not doing, grace emphasizes who we are in Jesus Christ.

4. People are accepted as they are. . . . God accepts us because we are His children in Christ. A grace-oriented church shows acceptance to people not only when they come to Christ for salvation, but also as they try to live the Christian life. Such a church accepts differences in culture, personality, opinion, giftedness, questionable matters, and personal preferences because God has accepted the person.

5. The unbiblical extremes of license and legalism are avoided. Grace is not perverted into an excuse to do whatever we please, called license. The Bible

says that grace teaches us to live godly lives. The opposite perversion of grace, legalism, implies that we must adhere to non-biblical or man-made standards to be acceptable to God. . . . [A] grace-oriented church holds to the Bible's clear teachings, is flexible in the unclear issues, and never allows human rules to supersede the authority of Scripture.

6. Liberty is balanced by love. . . . A grace-oriented church will teach how to balance the joyful liberty of the Christian life with a love for God and others. This means that in areas of conscience or questionable things, we are encouraged to temper our activity by considering how it will affect others and by acting only out of love.

7. There is an emphasis on being, not doing. Busyness is not godliness; godliness is godliness. And godliness begins in the heart with the realization of who we are as God's children through faith in Christ. The grace-oriented church encourages godliness by emphasizing growth in our personal relationship to God. Ministry and service come from the joyful desire to honor God, not the mistaken belief that God is not happy unless we are busy.

8. There is a sincere desire to share the message of grace. . . . If a church is seeking after God's heart, they will be active in reaching the world with the gospel of grace, because that is where God's heart is.

9. Those who sin are dealt with biblically. . . . Personal confession and restoration is taught. Sins of a more public or blatant nature are handled by the church lovingly and prayerfully with the goal of restoring the offender to full fellowship with God and the church. The grace-oriented church reflects a healing environment rather than a critical and condemning spirit.[16]

Third, a church must be **Christ-centered and biblically-grounded**. These aspects of a thriving church are indispensable.

Regarding *Christ-centeredness*, Jesus is not only the foundational "cornerstone" on which the Church is built (Eph. 2:20), but He's also the Rock on which our personal faith rests (Matt. 7:24–25; 1 Cor. 10:4). Our focus on Him must be unwavering. Paul went so far as to say "I decided that while I was with you I would forget everything except Jesus Christ, the one who was crucified" (1 Cor. 2:2). Similarly, the writer of Hebrews enjoined all of us to fix our eyes on Jesus, "the champion who initiates and perfects our faith. Because of the joy awaiting him, he endured the cross, disregarding its shame" (Heb. 12:2). In other words, the importance of everything in our life must pale in comparison to the importance of Jesus, our Savior.

As for *being biblically-grounded*, scripture has always been a fundamental part of Christianity, as far back as the ministry of Jesus, who quoted twenty-four books of the Hebrew scriptures. Then, after His ascension, the New Testament joined the Old Testament to instruct the faithful. As the early church father, Iranaeus (A.D. 130-202), explained, salvation came by those who preached the gospel, "but afterward, by the will of God, they delivered to us the Scriptures, to be for the future, the foundation and pillar of our faith" (*Against Heresies*, Bk. 3, Chap. 1). The place of scripture in any church must be paramount. "All Scripture is inspired by God," says Second Timothy 3:16, "and is useful to teach us what is true and to make us realize what is wrong in our lives. It corrects us when we are wrong and teaches us to do what is right." Nothing can be a substitute for God's Word—not inspiring traditions, not clever sermons, not amazing worship songs, not fun community events. It's by way of scripture that faith itself comes to those needing salvation (Rom. 10:17). It's also through the Bible that persons already following Christ receive everything needed "for living a godly life" (2 Peter 1:3).

Fourth, any church must be *a house of prayer*, as God declared in the Old Testament: "my Temple will be called a house of prayer for all nations"

(Is. 56:7). Jesus quoted this same verse when leveling His condemnation against those who had turned the Jerusalem synagogue into a den of thieves (Matt. 21:13). The great Reformer, Martin Luther (1483–1546), observed, "To be a Christian without prayer is no more possible than to be alive without breathing."

Fifth, every church should have a ministry that is **locally and globally involved** (see Chapter Three). This reflects the last command given by Jesus, who told His followers to "make disciples of all the nations, baptizing them in the name of the Father and the Son and the Holy Spirit." (Matt. 28:19). Charles Spurgeon (1834–1892), the famous nineteenth-century evangelist, explained with crystal clarity the seriousness of evangelism: "If there be anything about which we cannot tolerate lukewarmness, it is in the matter of sending the gospel to a dying world."[17]

To summarize, then, a good church should display at least three general principles of action: 1) connecting people to God (1 Peter 3:15; 1 John 1:3); 2) growing members to be faithful followers of Christ (Col. 1:28; Heb. 5:12–14, 6:1–4); and 3) sowing seeds of the Gospel while spreading the good news of God's Kingdom (Rom. 1:16).

## TAKE ONE STEP AT A TIME

Right about now you might be asking yourself: "Ok, now that I know how to find a *good* church, how do I find the *right* good church *for* me?"

The answer to this question isn't too complicated. There are several courses of action to take and many things to look for when trying to find a church right *for you*. Most basic is your need to be intentional and pro-active. You can't just sit around waiting for the right church to come along. Finding a church requires a plan that involves visiting local churches, talking to others, and maybe even doing some online research. It will certainly take a little time and effort, but it shouldn't be too difficult. Most of us have already made similar searches many times before: e.g., looking for a suitable home, trying to find a good gym, or hunting for a new job.

Of course, as with any project, there are certain hurdles we must overcome. The first involves information overload. I'm sure you know what I mean. All of us are inundated with daily podcasts, social media posts, blogs, streaming radio, cable TV, news alerts, and pop-up ads. Go here! Go there! Videos! Graphics! Do this! Do that! Glitz! Glamor! *This* church is amazing! *That* church is awesome! It can be dizzying and rather numbing. It can also leave us feeling disheartened, thinking, *Gee, my church isn't like that. We don't have nice big broadcast screens. And our activity center isn't half the size of the one at that church I saw on TV.*

But we must realize that in this era of polished presentations (especially those coming through TV or the Internet), we're not seeing all of the sweat and strain that goes into creating a final result. We're only seeing the finished product. So, remember this: When you first start looking for a church and find a place where perhaps everything is not-so-perfect, it means very little. Don't judge a book by its cover. Relax. Check it out. Have a good time. You must immerse yourself into a community to really see what's happening there.

You also need to change your thinking about church involvement. Instead of fixating on what God might want a certain *church* to do, you should concentrate more on what God might want *you* to do. Your responsibilities are a separate issue from what any church is doing (or not doing). And if there does happen to be some minor problems in a church you're attending, then focus on being a part of the solution to those problems. In other words, if a church isn't doing a good enough job, then it might actually mean that *you're* not doing a good enough job.

It's dysfunctional to keep complaining: "My church is not doing this. My church is not doing that. It's not meeting this need. It's not meeting that need." You must instead say, "I know there's no perfect church because every church is run by imperfect humans. But I can still be part of this church if it desires to honor God. I can join with imperfect pastors, staffers, and volunteers, as long as they're seeking God's glory. I can enjoy common ground and close connections with imperfect believers who, despite their shortcomings/failures, keep striving to serve God as best they can." If you can say these things, honestly, then it's indeed possible that you've already found the right church for you—not the *perfect* church, but the *right* church.

Where does God want me? What does God want me to do? These are the questions that you should ask when trying to find the *right* church, rather than the *perfect* church. It's true that everyone should find a church compatible with their own personality, desires for ministry, and unique talents/gifts. But in the end, it's not about us. We don't join a church to meet our needs. We join a church to further God's agenda. This is done by: sharing the gospel; discipling others; and meeting the needs of my neighbor (emotionally, spiritually, physically).

In other words, you can't go into a church with the idea: *What am I going to get out of this church that will help me?* We must keep our minds and hearts committed to another idea: *What am I going to put into this church that will make a difference in the lives of others?* This highlights a real danger facing millennials, who have been conditioned to live according to a consumerism mindset, which isn't God's way. God's way isn't about *getting*, it's about *giving*.

Obviously, if a church's mission doesn't align with your heart's calling and/or the passion God has placed in you, then it wouldn't be wrong to explore other churches that might be a better fit—as long as you keep in mind that not everyone receives a vision. Some people are visionaries. Others are field workers. Too many people leave what could be the *right* church for them just because that church's vision doesn't match what they feel *might* be their own vision. But God only gives visions to certain people. Others are created to adopt someone else's vision. If we're a field worker always insisting on *our* "vision," then we'll just end up isolating ourselves because we'll keep seeking our own desires, rather than God's true plan for us.

The best way to avoid this pitfall is to never forget: *It's not about me; it's not about what I can get. It's about what I can give.* This proper attitude reminds me of what was said by American president, John F. Kennedy (1917–1963), in his inauguration speech: "Ask not what your country can do for you; Ask what you can do for your country." Said in a more relevant way for us, "Ask not what your church can do for you; Ask what you can do for your church."

## HONOR THE BRIDE OF CHRIST

It's been rightly said that we must hate what God hates. But the reverse is also true. We must love what God loves. And God loves the Church. Jesus suffered for the Church, shed His blood for the Church, died on the cross for the Church. The Church, obviously, is very important to Jesus. And what's important to Him should also be important to us. This alone is enough reason for us to be plugged into a good church (a gathering of *the* Church). But there's another reason to find a good church. It's the tool God uses to fulfill His purpose and will on earth.

As noted earlier in this chapter, scripture metaphorically describes the Church as the spiritual "Body" of Christ (1 Cor. 12:27; Eph. 1:23). He's the head, while we are His hands, feet, eyes, and heart. As members of the Church, we actually reflect Jesus in a way similar to how Jesus reflected the Father: "Anyone who has seen me has seen the Father!" (John 14:9). Paul, in reference to himself, noted, "It is no longer I who live, but Christ lives in me" (Gal. 2:20). This truth, which has great power, is best presented to the world when we gather as a church and together do the work of the ministry. It's through us that Jesus continues His ministry/mission.

At this point you might be tempted to ask: "Why must I go to a building on Sundays to serve God? After all, I'm already in the Church because I'm a Christian." "Why can't I just serve God without going to some boring meeting with a bunch of strangers?" "Wouldn't it be better for me to actually be out there living for God instead of spending time at church?" "Instead of going to church, couldn't I just go out with friends to discuss God? Or, volunteer my time for a charity? Maybe I could even serve a meal to someone at a homeless shelter."

These are good questions, but they're all built on a faulty premise: i.e., that being part of a church is simply about fulfilling some command to go to a building on Sundays. But being part of a church is about far more than that. It's about being plugged into a *community*. Hebrews 10:25 instructs us to not stop "meeting together" in a community setting, as "some people do." This same verse tells us that we *need* to meet together so we can all encourage one another as we see "the day of his return is drawing near."

Another reason we need community is because we were created as communal creatures. God didn't make any lone wolves. Our lives aren't meant to be lived alone. Consider just about anything in life that requires action and you'll find that you can't do it alone. There must be others with whom you interact. This is how we were built to live. God uses interaction to mold us, shape us, and change us. A child left alone would turn out to be an extremely dysfunctional adult. So it is with us as Christians when we're born-again. We *need* others to grow properly.

Others also need *us*, especially now when so many churches seem to be full of false Christians, sinful leaders, and/or members who hold unbiblical views. Some people might argue, "I don't want to go to a church because of a bad experience at a church that still bothers me. Churches have too many hypocritical members and flawed leaders." This can be a difficult and painful hurdle to overcome, but a slight change in perspective might make a world of difference. Instead of focusing on what you've seen (or see) wrong/bad in others, focus on what is right/good in you, then seek to express that goodness/godliness with the hope of helping others to change. "Be an example to all believers in what you say, in the way you live, in your love, your faith, and your purity," Paul said (1 Tim. 4:12).

Moreover, people who attend a church with like-minded believers reap many benefits. They enjoy fellowship with each other, get support for ministry work, and receive assistance during difficult times. We also grow spiritually the more we interact with other believers. As Proverbs puts it, "Iron sharpens iron, so a friend sharpens a friend" (Prov. 27:17). Being in a church additionally gives us the chance to join with others in a common goal that, when tackled by many people, will likely be reached more easily and more quickly than if it had been pursued by only one person (e.g., feeding the hungry, spreading the gospel, caring for the sick). And, of course, it's in a church that we can become better equipped and empowered through discipleship training for whatever work we might want to do throughout the world.

Getting plugged into a good church is all about: a) becoming whoever God created you to be; and b) fulfilling whatever God has called you to do. Jesus emphasized this truth by praying that His followers would be "one" (John 17:11, 20–23). His prayer was answered immediately after He rose from the dead, as people expressed their faith, joined the church, and regularly came together under God's banner of love. Together they spread the gospel, cared for the needy, and made important decisions (Acts 2:1, 44–46, 4:31–32, 12:12, 14:27, 15:22, 30). Then, as the winds of time scattered members of the Church across Asia and Europe, the earliest believers soon recognized the greatest asset God had given them: each other.

Today, we have this same gift—the gift of other people. This is the precious treasure God has given us to use as we seek to accomplish whatever work He's called us to do. For it is to people we must turn as we build our *Team of Dreamers*, which is the subject of our next chapter.

## 2

# BUILD YOUR TEAM OF DREAMERS

God wants you to embrace His dream.
He also wants you on His team, because
it takes a team to fulfill His dream.

— Dale O'Shields —
Church of the Redeemer[18]

N ot long ago, when I was neck-deep in the monumental task of strategic planning, I was convinced that God was going to do great things, especially as I completed my plans to secure a ministry grant. Finally, after lots of work, I was done. So, with confidence I showed it to a member of my ministry team, believing he'd be as impressed and excited as I was. But all he said was, "That's not gonna get it done." Then, he began shredding my wonderful plan to pieces.

A rather heated discussion ensued. I was shocked, angry, and offended. I had worked so hard on making it perfect. I thought: *Wait a minute! This is the best thing I've ever come up with! All my business experience, background, and knowledge has created this thing. Can't he see that I've followed every step of planning—perfectly?* I had definitely checked all my steps, and I had properly listed the vision, values, methods, obstacles, and metrics. I was all set to proceed forward toward great things, until this "trouble-maker" stopped me dead in my tracks.

Gradually, as the days passed, I calmed down. I then spoke to several other people about the plan, discussed the situation with my wife, and prayed. Soon, I began seeing that my friend was right. My blindspots had produced several flaws in the plan; God had clearly sent His servant to reveal my errors. There was only one course of action. I told this godly friend that his points were absolutely valid and I re-adjusted my plan accordingly. The results were amazing. The ministry got far more accomplished following *God's* plan, than it would have gotten done following *my* plan. But I needed the help of my honest, direct, and respectful friend.

One reason our back-and-forth was possible was because we trusted each other. He trusted my leadership and vision; I trusted his character and commitment. He trusted that I'd weigh his suggestions honestly (once I calmed down); I trusted that he cared about my ministry plans. You must have this kind of relationship with your ministry team members. Any good ministry team will be a collection of partners whose judgement and input you trust/value. They should be people who you know will always put the success of God's work first; individuals who will lift you up, help you be your best, and present you in a right way to the world.

These will be the same people you'll be able to trust with sensitive information; these companions will give you good advice and counsel when it comes to big decisions. And this, as my story shows, will sometimes include disagreements. The last thing you want is someone who will always agree with you. One of the things most disturbing to me is when I lay out a plan, then ask if there are any questions, and nobody says anything. It makes me wonder: *Is it because they think it's perfect, or is it because they just don't want to cause conflict?* You want people to challenge you. At the same time, of course, you don't want someone eager to tear you apart if you make a mistake. You need a balanced team. Such people are all around you, trust me. But you must open your eyes to see them. God is faithful. He will always *appoint* people and *anoint* people to whom you can turn in complete trust as you seek to serve Him.

Trust, of course, is a multi-directional thing. You must not only trust your team members, but your team members must also trust you (as well as each other). You need to feel that whatever happens, you'll be able to rely on them. And they need to believe that if something goes wrong, they'll be able to rely on you (and each other). Everyone should have a sense of assurance that if the ball gets dropped, someone's going to pick it up!

People are going to want to be part of any ministry team that functions in such a way. You never want people walking away from your team (or your project) harboring that old cliché in their mind: *Wow! This ministry would have been great if it hadn't been for all the people!*

But how do you get a ministry team? And before reaching that point, how do you even find your ministry calling, then come up with a ministry plan by which you can serve the Lord? Well, read on. Because the rest of this chapter will cover the very first steps you must take in order to bring about your plans to serve God—or what I like to call, your God-given dream.

## FOLLOW YOUR GOD-GIVEN DREAM

Everyone dreams of doing something significant. And God makes those dreams possible by creating us with unique gifts, talents, and passions. The difficulty is figuring out the difference between a *personal* dream and a *God-given* dream.

Pursuing the former will never lead to complete fulfillment, nor bring about anything of eternal worth. Seeking the latter, however, will always result in godly satisfaction, an eternal legacy, and most importantly, God's glorification.

Now, to be honest, a lot of Christians get nervous when they hear talk about dreams, goals, successes, and achievements. That's understandable because secular teachers outside the church (and false teachers inside the church) use these same terms to promote the "self." But when I talk about receiving, cultivating, and succeeding at a dream, I'm not talking about anything that springs from one's own sinful desires or selfish goals. I'm talking about a dream, goal, or purpose that comes from God, a calling rooted and grounded in serving God for His glory. Louie Giglio, senior pastor of Passion City Church, puts it this way:

> Maybe your dream is to go to school or get a degree or accomplish a certain task or find a spouse or start a business or move to a certain place or create a movement or carry the gospel to people who've never heard it before. Those may be great dreams, but there's a bigger dream that overrides everything else: it's that your life counts for the glory of God. That's the overriding dream of God's heart. If we don't embrace that dream, then we are in trouble, because all our smaller dreams are subject to change.[19]

This is not to say we get *nothing* out of serving God. We receive abiding peace, boundless joy, ever-present comfort, and an eternal perspective on those things that have true meaning/value in life. These blessings can't be experienced, or even understood, by persons still trapped in the world, because unlike those in the world we think "about the things of heaven, not the things of earth" (Col. 3:2). We, as born-again believers, recognize that there are dreams, goals, hopes, and purposes that continue beyond the grave. And God has uniquely equipped us to achieve success in all these areas, not for our glory, but for *His* glory.

We are also blessed as we pursue our God-given dreams by the magnificent things that happen not just *around* us and *through* us, but also *within* us. Chasing after our God-given dream through ministry work is actually one of the best ways to mature and evolve into someone who is more like Christ. And this should be our ultimate dream—i.e., to let God transform you into a new person by changing the way you think (Rom. 12:2). It's a daily process. All of us, as we contemplate the Lord's glory, become "more and more like him as we are changed into his glorious image" (2 Cor. 3:18).

## PERFORM A REALITY CHECK

Here we must ask an obvious question: *How can I know the difference between a God-given dream and just some notion that popped into my head?* This is an important issue because I've seen far too many people pursue a certain "dream" for decades, yet achieve no success. I, too, have been sidetracked by chasing after what I thought was a God-given dream, only to discover it was simply an idea that rose out of my own desires (or excitement about something).

For instance, I used to be involved with music. I actually produced four CDs. I also led worship, wrote music, and sang for thousands! I thought music was what God wanted me to do. But then I realized that although my musical talent was good, it wasn't great. I couldn't function at a level high enough to succeed at a musical "dream." Music was *a* thing for me to do, but it wasn't *the* thing for me to do. Being a musician for God wasn't an evil dream, nor was it a sinful dream. On the contrary, it was an honorable dream. But it wasn't a dream for me from God.

It's easy to confuse one's own dream for a God-given dream, especially if it's a worthy goal (e.g., feeding the poor, leading worship, starting a children's ministry, going on mission trips). We must remember, however, that just because a dream is godly, that doesn't mean it came from God. But there are ways to test a dream. For instance, when God gives you a dream, He'll also give you the resources needed. After all, if He gives us our daily bread (Gen. 22:14; Matt. 6:11, 31–32; Phil. 4:19), it only makes sense that He'd also give us whatever we may need to fulfill His dream for us. And I'm not just talking about money. I'm talking about talents, opportunities, and perhaps most importantly, people.

Another way to distinguish between a self-inspired dream and a God-inspired dream is to identify who will get the glory. Is it you? Is it God? Jesus said, "Those who speak for themselves want glory only for themselves, but a person who seeks to honor the one who sent him speaks truth, not lies" (John 7:18). And in Isaiah 42:8, we read: "'I am the Lord; that is my name! I will not give my glory to anyone else, nor share my praise with carved idols.'" Anything can be an idol, even something that seems like a godly goal. So, you must be vigilant to walk humbly before God, knowing that both the dream and its success is from, and for, Him.

## BUILD YOUR DREAM TEAM

It might be true that alone we can move quickly, and in so doing, likely accomplish a great deal. But an even more crucial truth is that we'll always be able to do more with a good team sharing our burden; we need a team to help us see what we might otherwise miss. Even Jesus chose twelve disciples with whom he carried out His ministry. And at one point, when He sent them out to do ministry, He sent them in twos (Mark 6:7). As one African Proverb puts it, "If you want to go fast, go alone. If you want to go far, go together." Or, as Helen Keller observed, "Alone we can do so little; together we can do so much." Not only will you go a lot further and do much more when working with others, but you'll also be able to make your plans, negotiate your tasks, and ultimately reach your goals a lot easier. Everything will go smoother.

Building your dream team is one of the most, if not *the* most, important step you'll take in moving forward with your God-given dream. As Craig Groeschel—founder and senior pastor of Life.Church, the largest church in the United States—has insightfully noted: "The key to success in any organization is identifying, developing, and empowering the right people."[20] Only by building the right dream team will you reach your God-given dream. And the best way to start building that team is to surround yourself with people with similar goals, values, and attitudes—people willing to join your dream. I don't mean people who will follow you as if you're a commander and they're soldiers. I mean people sold out for God and who, as the Lord directs them, are willing to support your vision in hopes of winning the world to Christ.

I remember in 2015 when Levant Ministries launched its first NEXTGEN Conference (nextgenconference.org). People were absolutely amazed at how the team functioned. The event ran efficiently and professionally. At one point I even realized, much to my shock, that I was barely needed. I could have probably been totally removed from the conference and it would have still continued effortlessly. Everyone knew their job, accepted their responsibilities, respected each other's duties, and saw where/how they fit into the overall picture. I couldn't have been more proud of them. God was honored and glorified.

Obviously, finding the right team is very important. But how does one find the right team? Take out a wanted advertisement in the paper? Stand on a street corner with a big sign that says, "DREAMERS WANTED"? Staple posters to the side of abandoned buildings and on telephone poles? No, there is a much easier way to find your dream team. All you need to do is keep your eyes open for people who have certain qualities that make them right for your team.

## PURSUE A PASSION; DEVELOP A DREAM

At the outset, you need people who can get excited about your dream; you need people who have a passion similar to the one God's given you. They need to be able to stand by your side, shoulder to shoulder, and see what you see. They can't just stand in front of you and keep looking at you. If they do, then all they'll be seeing is you, not your God-given dream. Focusing only on you will distract them from God's vision, especially when/if problems arise during the work of the ministry. A real key to success, then, is the ability to inspire others to come alongside you so they can see and embrace God's vision. They need to share your dream, and see it as you see it.

At the very least, persons on your team should have a dream for their own life that fits into your dream. For instance, my dream is to empower the next generation of leaders. That's my dream. Someone else on the team, however, might have a dream about organizing conferences for missionary groups. Another person might have a dream to be a fundraiser for God-glorifying projects. And a third individual might have a dream to meet the administrative/secretarial needs of a ministry that is short-staffed. None of these people have my specific dream, but their dreams fit into my dream. Our dreams are complementary, which helps us all work as one to accomplish God's big-picture dream that brings everyone together.

In other words, you must find other *dreamers* who, like you, have received a God-ordained dream. Without other dreamers, you'll likely end up having only mediocre results. You need dedicated, sold-out-for-God, walking-with-Jesus believers who are secure in knowing that they have a God-ordained dream/ purpose. Find individuals who are actively engaged in seeking to succeed at whatever God has called them to do. Such people tend to aim higher, go farther, and work harder toward achieving a goal. They've resolved to do their best for God's glory.

Real dreamers often strive for exceptional results by going the extra mile, looking for new ways to succeed, and being ready to jump at every opportunity that might come up unexpectedly. Dreamers who are firmly convinced in their minds and hearts that God has given them a dream to pursue seem to always set the bar higher. And that's needed because, after all, we're not talking here about some materialistic endeavor that will result in nothing but temporal rewards. The goal is to change the world for Christ!

## HANDLE THE COMPLAINERS

An additional quality needed in members of a good team is positivity. Have you ever met someone who's irredeemably negative? No matter what the situation (or project) might be, they can only focus on what's wrong, wrong, wrong. They're like Eeyore in *Winnie the Pooh*, the depressed donkey for whom nothing is ever right. Such individuals can never get past all the problems, setbacks, and obstacles they see. It's almost as if a dark cloud follows them everywhere. Being realistic is one thing. That's necessary. We, in fact, desperately need realistic people around to keep us visionaries from getting carried away. But the Eeyores of the world go way beyond being realistic, habitually wallowing in the realm of pessimism. They'll never make *anything* happen because they've allowed themselves to be defeated even before trying.

Rather than building your team with people who only see problems, try surrounding yourself with people who are always up for discovering solutions. These people, interestingly, also tend to set big goals no matter how many hurdles they must overcome. This, too, can be very uplifting and inspirational. I love surrounding myself with people who dream boldly and who have big plans for the Kingdom. And I'm not referring here to those who are mere talkers. (A lot of people talk.) I'm referring here to real dreamers, who are also real *doers*! They act on their God-given dream, take steps to make it come true, and aggressively work to reach their goal.

A true dreamer, who is relying on God for strength, will always push beyond their limits in order to achieve the impossible. They fully embrace Paul's words: "Work willingly at whatever you do, as though you were working for the Lord rather than for people. Remember that the Lord will give you an inheritance as your reward, and that the Master you are serving is Christ" (Col. 3:23–24). It's a wonderful experience to be around people who dream big. As Pastor Craig Groeschel says, "For the sake of those who don't know Christ, think big."[21]

A similar sentiment has been expressed by Christine Cain, an Australian social/ Christian activist who in 2008 co-founded A21, an extraordinary organization that raises awareness of human trafficking throughout the world in order to "[a]bolish slavery everywhere, forever" and secure freedom "for every human being in the planet."[22] TALK ABOUT DREAMING BIG! If that's not dreaming big, then I don't know what is. What is Cain's advice? "Determine today that you are going to spend the rest of your life focused on the Bigness of

God, and through His eternal perspective, live your life for a purpose so much greater than yourself."[23]

## PROMOTE A SELFLESS AND SACRIFICIAL SPIRIT

There's an old saying in the corporate arena: *It's a dog-eat-dog world.* Basically, it means that in order to succeed you must be ruthless, selfish, uncaring, and willing to fight for survival, even if it means hurting others. This attitude is the very opposite of the kind of heart you want on your team. Look for people who put the interests of the team ahead of their own interests; find people who feel that advancement of *the team* is more important than advancement of *the self.*

*Selfless* ranks extremely high on the list of desirable qualities because neither a team, nor a dream, should ever depend on just one person. Any team that rests on just one person's shoulders will inevitably fall apart. Sadly, that's what we often see in today's churches. An entire ministry is built on, or built around, a single person. Then, when that person leaves for some reason (e.g., old age, illness, death, family responsibilities, perhaps even a personal problem), the whole ministry crumbles. So, when seeking team members, examine how each person is: a) contributing to the workload; b) helping others succeed; and c) putting the team's needs first.

*Sacrificial,* too, is an indispensable quality. Although related to selflessness, it has an extra component. Selfless is defined as "having or showing great concern for other people and little or no concern for yourself" (*Merriam-Webster Dictionary*) or being "concerned more with the needs and wishes of others than with one's own" (*Oxford Dictionary*). But sacrificial is defined as an act "involving sacrifice," which is the "destruction or surrender of something for the sake of something else, something given up or lost" (*Merriam-Webster Dictionary*). The

*Oxford Dictionary* gives an even more poignant meaning of sacrifice as being the "act of giving up something valued for the sake of something else regarded as more important or worthy."

Here is the essence of how every Christian should be viewing not just other members of a ministerial team, but also their family, friends, fellow believers, strangers, and unbelievers. A *sacrificial* attitude goes beyond selflessness, into a realm where a person puts the needs of others ahead of their own, and does so to the point of it costing them something valuable: time, money, energy, and in some cases, life itself. Our Lord taught, "There is no greater love than to lay down one's life for one's friends" (John 15:13). He then showed what he meant by dying for the world.

## INVEST TIME, TREASURE, AND TALENT

Finally, a leader must accurately assess the time, treasure, and talent of any potential team member. How much time can someone dedicate? How much treasure (e.g., finances, networking connections, personal equipment) can someone invest? How much talent can a person offer? I'm *not* saying you should only seek the smartest, most talented, wealthiest, or most experienced people for your team. That would be contrary to scripture, which tells us that God often uses the opposite of what the world seeks. He uses the *foolish* to confound the wise, and the *weak* to bring down the strong (1 Cor. 1:27). I'm only pointing out that time, treasure, and talent should be noted when organizing a specific team for a specific dream. For instance, if you're forming a team to build a school, it would be good to know that there's an architect who wants to get involved in ministry. It would also be good to know about another person who works as a corporate fundraiser.

Time, treasure, and talent all fall under the umbrella term "availability." Notice that I use the term "availability," rather than "ability." I do this because God is not as concerned with *ability* as he is about *availability*. The difference is subtle, but significant. A person with *ability* has just that (i.e., a deep well of resources from which they can pull many assets to contribute to a team). However, someone with *availability* not only possesses certain assets, but they also possess a desire to offer those assets for the work of God's kingdom to bring Him glory.

Availability also raises the issue of perseverance, which is yet another key characteristic to consider when picking team members. I've organized many teams for many different kinds of projects. And one thing I've noticed is that some people simply can't stay the course. They initially get excited about a project, especially when I give out assignments. They'll run full speed ahead with their responsibilities for a week (or two) . . . or for a month (or two). But at some point they lose interest. Suddenly, their availability begins to diminish, until one by one their tasks are not being done. It's sad and disappointing to watch because I know such persons will miss out on great blessings. We must never "get tired of doing what is good," said Paul. "At just the right time we will reap a harvest of blessing if we don't give up" (Gal. 6:9).

## EXPAND YOUR CAPACITY

The main purpose of Levant Ministries is to share the Gospel with Arabic-speaking people of the Middle East, while simultaneously: a) equipping believers; and b) mobilizing the next generation of leaders to extend the local/global reach of the Church. By God's grace we've placed teams in Jordan, Egypt, Lebanon, Canada, and the United States. And throughout all of our operations we've been blessed with literally hundreds of volunteers, who have committed themselves to working for God through the dream of Levant Ministries. This is how I, too, started out in ministry (i.e., as a volunteer). Eventually, however, I felt moved by God to leave my secular career behind and start my own team of dreamers.

As I've previously noted, finding the right team members to help you succeed at your God-given dream is crucial. The qualities you want to see in them include: a passion/dream, a good attitude, a selfless/sacrificial heart, and availability. But every leader must also possess their own special qualities to be effective. They must be able to clearly communicate with the team, stay committed to their dream, remain connected to God, and be caring of their flock. All of these things reflect the fruit of the Holy Spirit: "love, joy, peace, patience, kindness, goodness, faithfulness, gentleness, and self-control" (Gal. 5:22–23). If any of these qualities are not present in a leader, then they must be cultivated immediately.

## COMMUNICATE WITH YOUR TEAM

My first step toward full-time ministry was to share my dream with potential team members. And I quickly learned that there is a supernatural power released when any God-given dream is shared. Much to my surprise, I was soon able to recruit hundreds of volunteers. The dreamers who joined me saw a vision they could support; they were drawn to a dream based on the gospel and God. (Many leaders, by the way, forget that every dream must be all about God.)

*So, don't sleep on your dreams. Wake up and share your dreams with the world.* This is what leaders do. They share their hearts, visions, hopes, and even fears. A team must be built on truths shared openly, even if they're difficult to bear. That's a leader's responsibility. It has to be done for the good of the team and dream. Christ, our example, demonstrated this leadership principle when he pulled his disciples aside, saying: "'Listen, we're going up to Jerusalem, where all the predictions of the prophets concerning the Son of Man will come true. He will be handed over to the Romans, and he will be mocked, treated shamefully, and spit upon. They will flog him with a whip and kill him, but on the third day he will rise again'" (Luke 18:31–33).

Can you imagine hearing that plan? But look at the results. All Jesus had was a small, ragtag, undisciplined team of mostly fisherman, a few tradesmen, and a tax collector. Yet these men, after the darkest days they had ever known, changed the world! Like Jesus, a good NextGen leader must be able to clearly/concisely inform potential team members (and those already on a team) of the dream to be pursued. One must articulate not only the *overall* goal, but also the *specific* goals connected to the responsibilities and positions of each team member.

The success of any project will often depend almost entirely on the clarity and completeness of your communication with your team. Nothing can bring down a team's morale quicker than confusion over what needs to be done. Poor communication will always result in frustration. And before long, people will start dropping away—not because they don't want to help, and not because it's a bad/boring dream, but simply because they don't know what to do. It becomes too stressful to stay. There will be times, of course, when some members do leave. But don't be discouraged. Move forward. The best is yet to be. God is faithful.

## COMMIT TO YOUR DREAM

You need to be convinced of your dream. As Pastor Johnny Hunt of First Baptist Church told me, you have to see it to see it. Or, stated negatively, *If you don't see it, before you see it, you'll never see it.* In other words, you must have a visible goal and be resolute in your commitment to it. Don't get sidetracked. Follow everything through to a successful completion. You need to truly own it, day-in and day-out. Think of your dream like it's nourishment to your body: drink it, eat it, swallow it, and digest it as if your life depended on it.

This is not out-of-the-ordinary or extreme thinking by the standards of any successful person, whether they are a musician, healthcare worker, or business professional. It takes total dedication to be successful in any field. So, think of it this way: *If worldly people can show dedication to their dreams/goals for only temporary benefits in this world, how much more should Christians be able to show at least an equal amount of dedication to God's dream/goals for eternal benefits in the Kingdom of Christ!*

This puts everything into perspective for me. Interestingly, it's often when you begin showing your commitment to your dream that God starts sending other dreamers your way to help you. People suddenly identify with you and align with you. As they hear you speak, they want to assist you. Your dream catches on. By sharing your dream, God is able to move in the hearts of others, inspiring them to join with you to accomplish His will.

## CONNECT TO GOD

The most important thing to keep in mind when seeking to discover your dream, or when you're pursuing your dream, is that you'll succeed only if you're closely connected to God. . . I'm going to say that again . . . *only if you're closely connected to God.* One of my favorite promises from God is in James 4:8, "Come close to God, and God will come close to you. Wash your hands, you sinners; purify your hearts, for your loyalty is divided between God and the world." How do you get close to God? That depends. After Bible-reading, prayer, and fellowship, there's no set course for staying connected to God. Everyone is different.

Many people experience a deeper connection to God when they spend time quietly enjoying nature. Others feel closer to the Lord when they're listening to, playing, or even creating music. And some Christians, ironically, hear God's voice speaking most clearly amid the hustle and bustle of people rushing around a busy city. The many and varied ways that people stay closely connected to God are limitless. *How* you stay connected to God is really not that important. *That* you stay connected to God is crucial. He is the source of everything we need for a fulfilling, meaningful, and successful life. This is especially true when it comes to guidance.

It's terribly sad when a person is either pursuing the wrong dream, or pursuing no dream at all, simply because they're not clinging to God for direction. When Jesus was teaching about God's provision for His people, the principle He applied was "Seek the Kingdom of God above all else, and live righteously, and he will give you everything you need" (Matt. 6:33).

Jesus is clearly giving us our priorities. We must seek God before seeking anything else, including any dreams. It's from God that all good and perfect gifts come (James 1:17), including the gifts of guidance, direction, and passion for a specific work of ministry. And the only way to receive those gifts is to stay close to the gift-giver. Far too many people fixate on getting input from, and staying connected to, everyone *except* God (e.g., their pastors, other believers, Christian authors, radio/TV preachers). But those who primarily rely on these sources will only end up with someone else's dream. They'll miss the dream God specifically designed for them.

## CARE FOR YOUR FLOCK

A team leader must know their flock like any good shepherd knows his sheep. Remember Christ's words, "I am the good shepherd; I know my own sheep, and they know me" (John 10:14). A true relationship must exist between a shepherd and his sheep. You, as the team leader, must get to know each person on your team: their skills, gifts, passions, experiences, strengths, weaknesses, and thought processes. Study them. Talk to them. Listen to them.

At the same time, you must share with them information about yourself so they can get to know you. Your team of dreamers must feel as comfortable about you as you feel about them. You must help them gain an understanding of you as a Christian, a minister of the gospel, a leader, and a friend. Tell them about your experiences, what you feel, how you think, and where you stand on various issues. When Jesus built His team of disciples, He said, "Come and see" (John 1:39). Then, He exposed them to His ministry, heart, teachings, and life. Eventually, after an extended period of time together, He finally revealed His glorious purpose (Luke 9:22).

Getting to know your team, while your team simultaneously gets to know you, is imperative, especially when it comes to team members who have not yet reached their full potential. I'm constantly trying to uncover any potential that lies unrecognized in my team members. And there is often a lot to be found. I'm very intentional about it, making sure to always look for new abilities and strengths by giving them additional tasks and talking to them about how they feel about those tasks. And like most other aspects of working on a team, this practice should also be a two-way street. You should pray that God brings people into your life (and onto your team) who will help you find your own as-yet-undiscovered talents/gifts. God often uses a team to reveal all kinds of hidden potential in both you and your team members.

## MAKE IT HAPPEN

Becoming a NextGen leader isn't something that magically occurs overnight. There are steps to walk, and a path to take, toward whatever accomplishments God may have in store for you. It requires a lot of molding, shaping, and pruning of the self in order to get to where you finally: a) see *what* God wants you to do; and b) realize *how* He wants you to do it.

First, you must comprehend that you're actually part of the generation to whom God will one day entrust the future of His Church. This means that the Lord *has been* working, *is* working, and *will continue* to work in your life to prepare you for leadership. But until your time comes to lead, your responsibility is to humbly yield to God's preparation of your heart, mind, and spirit. "So humble yourselves under the mighty power of God, and at the right time he will lift you up in honor" (1 Peter 5:6). God is in charge of the training; you are responsible for the learning.

Second, you must move forward in faith, believing that God will guide you to where you need to go. Imagine yourself taking a road trip and you're the one who's driving. You must get yourself in the car, buckle up, pull out of the parking space, and start going down the road. If you were to never start driving, you would never go anywhere. There's a big difference, however, between a normal trip and a journey directed by the Lord. On a divinely-ordained adventure, although you're the one driving, it's God who is steering you toward your destination.

Third, you must embrace the belief that God will indeed do wonderful things to impact/advance the Kingdom through your efforts. Why is this mindset important? Because there's great power, motivation, and strength in believing your efforts *today* will ultimately have a great impact *tomorrow*. Having such a positive outlook can be extraordinarily encouraging in difficult times. So, don't be afraid to envision the future results of your labors (e.g., more souls saved, young disciples growing in Christ, new churches being planted, communities all over the world being changed for Jesus). Go ahead and dream about your dream. There are no limits when it comes to what God can accomplish through you and your godly team of dreamers. People will be changed. God will be glorified. Souls will be saved. Miracles will happen.

Sometimes the greatest miracles will involve those you choose for your team. In scripture we often see God using the most unlikely vessels to accomplish His will. Imagine building a team using the still-unknown Timothys, Johns, and Peters of tomorrow.

There are also the Pauls of tomorrow yet to be found, saved, and discipled. I often imagine finding a Paul in my work throughout the Middle East. Remember that Paul, originally named Saul, "was going everywhere to destroy the church. He went from house to house, dragging out both men and women to throw them into prison" (Acts 8:3). He also was at the murder of Stephen, Christianity's first martyr, as "one of the witnesses, and he agreed completely with the killing of Stephen" (Acts 8:1). By his own words, Paul admitted, "I persecuted the followers of the Way, hounding some to death, arresting both men and women and throwing them in prison. The high priest and the whole council of elders can testify that this is so. For I received letters from them to our Jewish brothers in Damascus, authorizing me to bring the followers of the Way from there to Jerusalem, in chains, to be punished" (Acts 22:4–5).

In today's terms, Saul would likely be termed a terrorist. But the Lord changed him into Paul. Might God still do such a miracle? Yes! I've personally seen the Holy Spirit transform former members of Al Qaeda, ISIS, and other extremist groups in the Middle East. Can you imagine such people being turned into church planters, worship leaders, or pastors!? Well, God is already doing it. Today, we have pastors Mohammed, Ali, Ahmed, and others all over the world. And their message as followers of Christ is radically different from their message as terrorists.

This difference was articulated in a 2014 sermon ("ISIS and Christ: Culture of Death and Culture of Life") delivered in Cairo, Egypt by Dr. Maher Samuel (Ravi Zacharias International Ministries). Dr. Samuel, one of our 2017 NEXTGEN Conference speakers, is an incredibly dynamic evangelist in the Middle East. Through his Antioch Project in the Middle East, he's taught thousands of Arabic-speaking Christian physicians and healthcare professionals how to share their faith and unveil the love of God at the bedsides of the sick and dying. According to Dr. Samuel, both ISIS and Christ hold out the "sovereignty of God," but with some vast differences:

They want to enforce the sovereignty of God through death. But Jesus offers the sovereignty of God through life. They use the sword to force people to submit to the sovereignty of God. But Jesus hung on the cross so that every person could submit willingly to the sovereignty of God. They want to subjugate people to submit to God. But Jesus gives people life so that they are free to choose the sovereignty of God.[24]

Like Dr. Samuel, you must realize that there are many different kinds of wildly conflicting options being offered in the world: e.g., alternative religions, various cults, atheism, humanism, and an assortment godless lifestyles that exalt the self. But there's hope for everyone. No one is beyond the possibility of being rescued by Jesus Christ through the power and presence of the Holy Spirit. And you can participate in Christ's ultimate victory by simply embracing a personal vision of ministry wherein you become an ambassador of His love.

Such a commitment to a God-given dream can be incredibly inspiring to others watching you; others, who, like you, might still be searching for their own God-given dream. Your actions now, at this very moment, could end up being an amazing gift to others who are seeking to serve God and who are wanting to do His work locally/globally—i.e., *glocally*. There is so much work to be done worldwide, beginning on a local level and extending out globally. This will be the subject of Chapter Three.

---- **3** ----

# EMBRACE A
# GLOCALIZED VISION

Of the 7.2 billion people alive in the world today,

3 billion of them live in unreached people groups with little

or no access to the Gospel of Jesus Christ. According to Joshua Project,

there are approximately 16,300 unique people groups in the world

with about 6,500 of them considered unreached.

— Global Frontier Missions —

I've always had a great love for the world, even throughout the earliest days of my Christian walk. And although I instantly felt a real concern for everyone, a very special place had been carved into my heart for my brothers and sisters still in the Middle East. My thoughts about them reflect a rather poignant segment of the blockbuster movie, *Titanic*, a film that chronicled the horrible tragedy of April 15, 1912, when 1,500 people died. The supposedly unsinkable *Titanic* went down to the bottom of the ocean only two hours and forty minutes after hitting an iceberg. Almost all of the passengers perished in the Atlantic's freezing depths because they were unable to get into the lifeboats—and many of those lifeboats were half-empty! Sadly, only a few of the lifeboats that got away bothered to return to save the survivors floundering in the water.

When I compare this terrible scene to my own life, I'm reminded of how God saved me after bringing me to America. I not only met Christ as my Savior, but I received an education, was given access to new technology, and was blessed with the kind of freedom I never would have known back home. He even blessed me with a wonderful secular career, before calling me into full-time ministry. It was as if God had put me in a lifeboat and taken me away from the disaster called the Middle East. But unlike those in the *Titanic* lifeboats, who remained at a safe distance, I want to go back to the Arab world to look for survivors. Now, I have a motto of sorts that I often share: *Just as a few half-empty lifeboats returned to rescue the freezing survivors of the Titanic, Levant Ministries is called to rescue people into the lifeboat of Jesus Christ.*

Every NextGen leader should have such a mindset. As I discussed in Chapter One, we certainly need to be in a good local church, but we must also be ever-mindful of the world beyond our community. Involvement in a local church is only part-one of a two-part story. We must be *local* leaders with a *global* perspective that is continually being developed in our hearts, cultivated by our activities, and pursued through our goals. This was how Jesus organized his Kingdom work. He built his team using local believers, then turned them into global leaders. We, too, must have love not only for our local community, but also for the entire world.

Many churches, however, are stuck in having only a local vision. Church leaders are admirably committed to things like evangelism outreaches in their home city, feeding the poor of their communities, visiting local hospitals or refugee camps, and lending help to the sick in surrounding neighborhoods. But when it comes to going beyond the borders of their home region, there's a stunning lack of programs or projects. A church can easily fall into the trap of obeying Christ's command to do the work of the Kingdom locally (i.e., in Jerusalem), while failing to extend that work outwardly to "Judea, in Samaria, and to the ends of the earth" (Acts 1:8). Yet this is the Great Commission: "Therefore, go and make disciples of all the nations, baptizing them in the name of the Father and the Son and the Holy Spirit" (Matt. 28:19).

## BECOME A GLOCALIZED LEADER

Glocalization is a fairly new concept. The term, in fact, still doesn't appear very often in mainstream literature, even though a 2011 *Financial Times* article was boldly titled, "Glocalization Rules the World."[25] The idea was popularized throughout the business environment of the 1990s. It described an updated method of product marketing/distribution being utilized by various corporations; most notably, Sony, which used the term *global localization* "in corporate advertising and branding strategies in the 1980s and 1990s."[26] The word glocalization, however, didn't appear until after an apparent mistranslation of the Japanese *dochakuka* ("becoming deeply rooted)." It was rendered "glocal" in a 1990 *U.S. News & World Report* article as a "word to watch." It was defined as "the trend among multinational corporations of dispersing power from their headquarters to far-flung branch offices."[27]

Another origin of the word emerged from the social sciences, specifically, "ecological efforts to connect the global and local in order to create awareness and enhance rethinking of frames of action."[28] It was used in reference to an exhibition piece—a three-dimensional orthogonal cube, called Rubik's Cube of Ecology—at the opening of the Global Change Exhibition (May 1990) in the Chancellery in Bonn, Germany.

> The main objective was to offer a representation of links along and across spatial scales in relationship to the goal of developing bridges relating local, to regional, to national, to global levels for the purposes of environmental research and management. Dr. Manfred Lange, the director of the touring

exhibit development team at that time and head of the German National Global Change Secretariat, called the depth dimension of this cube glocal in order to give a word for the magnitude ranging from micro [short-range], to meso [medium-range], to macro [long-range] scales.[29]

Yet a third origin for *glocalization* dates back to sociologist Roland Robertson, who used the term in the late 1980s. He formulated the concept at the same time as the Japanese using *dochakuka*. As he explains, "I was greatly struck in the early 1990s by learning that something similar to the term glocalization—namely, *dochakuka* (roughly, indigenization)—was being used in Japanese business practices, in reference to the ways in which goods or services are produced and, more important, distributed according to particularistic, local criteria."[30]

I'm reminded of Romans 8:28: "God causes everything to work together for the good of those who love God and are called according to his purpose for them." It seems that God can even use secular concepts (like glocalization) for His own purposes, even when those original concepts have nothing to do with God. Glocalization's idea of "dispersing power" to all corners of the globe from a local base, as well as its notion that there exists a deep inter-connectedness between short, medium, and long-range activities relating to the preservation of what is valued, perfectly fits Christian ministry! It represents, in the words of Pastor Bob Roberts, Jr. (Northwood Church), "the seamless integration between the local and global."[31]

Unfortunately, a lot of people who hear me talk about this "Glocalized Vision" in relation to the gospel immediately think: *It's too much. It's too big of a task. There's no way I can do this. There's no way that my church can do this.* But that's not faith talking. It's just fear. Faith understands that although glocal work can look terribly overwhelming, with the right view of God and the right outlook of the world, a glocalized dream/vision is achievable. And the amount of fruit that is now ripe for harvesting is incalculable, especially in areas of the world such as the Levant region of the Middle East, which is my primary area of ministry. There, despite a host of terrible and terrifying conditions, God has remained in the midst of His people. He's still moving. He's still saving the lost. He's still changing lives.

When it comes to the Levant, if only a tenth of those living in that area were to accept Jesus as their Lord and Savior, it would change the course of the Middle East. If Christianity's impact were to be even greater, it would likely change the course of the entire world! Consider, for example, Amal Bitar, a Syrian native from Hama. I met Amal at the language learning center for refugees in Sweden during one of our mission trips to reach out to refugees in Europe. During my interview with her, she shared her testimony with me on camera, speaking our native Arabic.

Amal was a teacher of some renown, having been picked by Asma al-Assad—Syria's First Lady—to end unemployment in Syria by teaching entrepreneurship to girls aged fifteen to nineteen. But when the Syrian Civil War broke out and ISIS invaded her land, everything for Amal changed. Life as she knew it was being destroyed around her as warfare was drawing ever-nearer to her home. She knew that staying in her country would mean certain death. So, she fled Syria, cautiously made her way to Lebanon, and then moved on to Turkey.

In Turkey, Amal paid $800 to book a seat on a boat she was told would take her to safety in Greece (to the island of Lesbos). All seemed to be going as planned until the boat came within about 50 yards of shore, at which point the captain of the vessel began throwing men, women, and children overboard. As it turns out, the man they'd all trusted to get them to safety was a smuggler. And once he had gotten close to shore, he began fearing the authorities. One by one, his human cargo went over the side into the rough waters of the Aegean Sea.

Crashing wave after crashing wave nearly drowned Amal. But then, by God's grace, a huge wave finally pushed her exhausted body to shore, where she was rescued by onlookers. Although Amal survived this terrifying ordeal, others have not been so lucky. Thousands have died in the Aegean Sea from exposure or drowning since the beginning of illegal transportations of refugees from Turkey, Syria, Afghanistan, Libya, and Iraq. In 2016 alone, nearly 3,800 died, including many young children and babies. Hedayetullah Habivyar from Afghanistan, for instance, lost his entire family: two children and his wife, who was in the last stages of her pregnancy. "I don't know why I'm alive," Hedayetullah sobbed to a news crew interviewing him after his rescue. "I have lost my whole family! What's left for me?"

Hedayetullah's heart-breaking story is only one of thousands. Fortunately for Amal, she was able to continue her journey after a brief recovery, ultimately finding safety in Sweden. It was there, in the shelter of a Christian Church, that Amal heard the gospel and accepted Jesus as her personal Lord and Savior. She immediately knew that God had a plan for her, just as He had promised through Jeremiah the prophet: "'For I know the plans I have for you,' says the Lord. 'They are plans for good and not for disaster, to give you a future and a hope'" (Jer. 29:11).

God's plan, Amal decided, was for her to serve Christ using her talents as a linguist and a teacher. She learned to speak Swedish in three short months!

Afterward, she began teaching the language to refugees at a language learning center. Thanks to that position, she gradually became rather well known. And through her notoriety, she was able to begin sharing her testimony and spreading the good news of Jesus. To this day, Amal continues to proclaim the love of Christ to the countless refugees flocking to Sweden, lost souls in need of a savior.

There are so many souls longing for Christ to deliver them. I'm reminded, for instance, of Muhammad, a man who called the Al Hayat Ministries television show "Without Shackels" (*Belakoyood* in Arabic). He had a pleading message to impart to viewers: "I hope that you will pray for our families in Iraq, so we can get rid of this great sadness that is now in Iraq. And from this terrorism, from this killing. It has hurt me a lot." Muhammad then revealed what he meant by being hurt. "My son was an engineer. And he was killed—he was beheaded."

The program's host, Katia, a good friend of mine and one of our 2017 NEXTGEN Conference speakers, flinched as her eyes filled with pity for this man's loss.

Muhammad continued his tragic tale with yet another heart-wrenching detail. "They recorded it and sent me the video—he was beheaded."

Katia shook her head, looking down in anguished disbelief. "We are sorry for what happened." What else could she say? She could only listen as Muhammad shared his story.

"You know, he was my only son." Muhammad's voice cracked with grief. "They killed my only son, my only son."

"I'm sorry, Brother Muhammad."

"They killed; they beheaded my only son. I raised him like a flower, as you would raise a rose. . . . All he was, was an engineer."

Katia kept listening, wanting to comfort Muhammad, but at a clear loss for words, until the conversation turned in an unexpected direction.

This broken man, in the midst of his crushing pain, suddenly said he'd been thinking about becoming a Christian. He had apparently learned about Jesus from some Christian neighbors. He wanted to join God's family, but was still a bit apprehensive because, as he explained it, "there has been enough killing and slaughtering."

Katia replied, "Do you know, Brother Muhammad, that God loves you in a special way, and has prepared for you a plan of salvation through the blood of Christ on the cross so that you don't have to carry the weight of sin and the worry of eternal life?"

Muhammad listened intently over the phone, remaining silent, as Katia continued to speak. "He has prepared salvation from sin and eternal life for you. All you have to do is accept Him today."

"I would love to," said Muhammad. "I would love to."

Then, together they prayed: "My loving God, I come before you today, and I open my heart. Pour your love, my God, into my heart. In the name of Jesus, save me from all my sins, forgive my trespasses, and help me live your will. Help me love you and love your people. And forgive everyone who has harmed me—even the ones who committed the crime of murder. I thank you, Lord, because you saved me from death. And that you wrote my name in the Book of Life. To you be the praise and glory in the name of Jesus, forever. Amen."[32]

## USE A HIGH-TECH GOSPEL

The musical *Jesus Christ Superstar* contains a very interesting song performed by Judas, wherein the betrayer of our Lord asks why Jesus decided to show up when there was no "mass communication." It's an understandable question. Spreading news during the first century was no easy task. There were only two means of communication in Jesus' day: 1) face-to-face discussions; or 2) the written word, using a sharp stylus/quill on a papyrus scroll, on a roll of leather, or on a little wooden tablet coated with wax. Can you imagine how time-consuming it must have been to share even the simplest message in writing?

No wonder Paul, in addition to writing his letters, decided to travel and preach in person. And he did so, despite the fact that ancient travel was arduous, dangerous, and slow. Even on the sturdiest of Roman roads, soldiers could march only about four to five miles per hour. Non-military personnel usually kept a three-miles-per-hour pace. This means that in a seven-hour day the average person could only go about twenty miles, while highly trained soldiers could reach around thirty to thirty-five miles. In other words, "Peter's trip from Joppa to Caesarea, a distance of 40 miles, took two days (Acts 10:23–24). Paul traveled from Troas to Assos on foot, a distance of about 20 miles (Acts 20:13–14), so it probably took him a day."[33]

Nevertheless, the gospel spread with miraculous speed. Beginning with only twelve disciples (including Matthias, who replaced Judas), the message of Christ filled Jerusalem, then spread throughout the Middle East, until finally extending into Europe and Asia Minor. Paul, sometimes called the thirteenth disciple (or last disciple), "clocked up around 10,000 miles traveling across the Roman Empire [by land *and* sea]"[34] before being brought back as a prisoner to Rome, where he was beheaded. All of the disciples, except John, were martyred. But these deaths didn't stop the gospel. "Almost one third of the Roman Empire became Christian in little more than 100 years."[35]

Think about how much more effectively the gospel can now be shared using today's many forms of high-tech communication! Unlike those who sought to share the message of Christ 2,000 years ago, we have TV, cable, the internet, digital recording devices (audio/video), high-speed printing, information storage solutions, and telecommunications. How could any Christian, especially a NextGen leader, not be passionate about using the various high-tech methods of communication at our disposal to participate in a glocalized vision/dream. The possibilities are limitless. If NextGen leaders were to all mobilize in a truly committed way to spread the gospel, the entire world could theoretically be reached in the very near future.

Consider this scenario: If we only had twelve believers in the world today, and each of those believers made just one convert in a year, the next year there would be twenty-four Christ followers. Then, if that twenty-four would then make only one convert, there would be forty-eight believers. Now, let's just suppose that such a rate of conversion were to continue every year—i.e., each believer would simply make one convert a year. If that were to happen, then in a mere thirty years the entire globe would be reached. This is an incredible statistic to ponder.

Is this too ambitious? Is this too unrealistic? Some believe so. But given the extraordinary power of today's communication methods, it might not be as farfetched an idea as it sounds. At the very least, NextGen leaders must recognize the amazing opportunities and possibilities now accessible because of technological tools that the early church didn't possess. And as we move forward in time, thanks to technology, the gospel will continue to spread much faster and farther. But the next generation must be active. They must be willing to use the many gifts of technology at our disposal, including Facebook, Twitter, and Instagram.

Everyone has a sphere of influence much larger than any of the first disciples possessed. It's up to us to decide whether or not to use our platform to reflect God's love, grace and mercy.

## BE A DISCIPLE-MAKER

One need look no further than the daily news reports to see that humanity is in desperate need of help and healing. Horrifying episodes of terrorism are occurring everywhere, economic markets are extremely volatile, war looms on the horizon of several countries, and the political landscape (especially in America) has become wildly unpredictable. What's the answer? Only Christ and His message of peace and love can alleviate such worldwide turmoil.

Sharing the gospel is obviously a priority. But Christians should be equally concerned, if not more so, with making disciples. This is the key to Christ's Church achieving a widespread glocalized vision of love, as Paul taught: "You have heard me teach things that have been confirmed by many reliable witnesses. Now teach these truths to other trustworthy people who will be able to pass them on to others" (2 Tim. 2:2). If every believer were to engage in disciple-making, the Great Commission would be fulfilled much faster. Unfortunately, too many people think that fulfilling the Great Commission just means making converts. But if we're not also making disciples and fellow disciple-makers, then the gospel will not go very far.

What exactly is discipleship? Using more modern terms, it's coaching or mentoring—nothing strange, nothing new, and nothing complicated. In fact, we see a perfect model of discipleship in the relationship between Paul and Timothy. Through their interactions we learn that there are at least three stages to discipling (coaching/mentoring): *parenting, pacesetting,* and *partnering.* This observation comes from Pastor Rick Warren (Saddleback Church).[36]

The first stage, *parenting,* relates to how a disciple-maker (as well as his/her disciple) understands the value of the past. Everyone must grow in Christ, just as a child grows in knowledge and wisdom. No good parent would simply leave a baby or a child alone and say, "Take care of yourself!" And one critical aspect of a child's growth is learning from the past experiences, insights, thoughts, and observations of a parent. In the area of Christian mentoring, this would not only involve a sharing of information/knowledge from mentor to disciple, but also a delving into the lives and observations of church leaders from long ago. It's recommended that "at least 25% of a church leader's reading be spent in pre-Reformation era writings," another 25% of reading should be "from the Reformation to the modern missionary age," 25% should "be drawn from the generation just previous to ours and only the remaining 25% among contemporary authors."[37]

The second stage, *pacesetting,* involves a mentor teaching by example. In his final exhortation to Timothy, Paul wrote, "you, Timothy, certainly know what I teach, and how I live, and what my purpose in life is. You know my faith, my patience, my love, and my endurance. You know how much persecution and suffering I have endured" (2 Tim. 3:10–11). How did Timothy know all of these things? Because he had joined himself to Paul and experienced life with him. You can do this same thing by simply signing up for a ministry in your local church. It's the quickest way to not only acquire a coach, but begin the discipleship process. Watch how the leader acts under stress. Pay attention to why the leader makes certain decisions. Listen to the leader's heart for ministry. Every NextGen leader must go through a period of following *today* in order to be properly equipped for leading *tomorrow*:

> [Paul] did not join their direction in life but rather invited them to join him in his direction. Likewise, Jesus did not start following the disciples, asking Peter and John when it would be convenient for them for him to stop by and give them the eight magical steps to be better fishermen. Rather, Jesus told them to follow him so he could teach them to advance his kingdom. The disciples joined Jesus' mission and direction in life, Jesus didn't join their mission and direction in life.[38]

The third stage, *partnering*, highlights that step when a disciple becomes a joint-leader, which is the final step before becoming a full-fledged leader. Evidence for this graduation appears in Romans 16:21, where Paul casually says, "Timothy, my fellow worker, sends you his greetings." Did you catch that: *my fellow-worker?* Timothy was no longer a disciple in the strictest sense of the word. He had become a fellow-leader, who would in time replace Paul and have disciples of his own. As Daniel Fusco, lead pastor at Crossroads Community Church, has observed: "A disciple is a learner. We are called to be disciples of Jesus and our relationships within the body of Christ should be geared so that all of us learn more and more about, and from, Jesus. . . . Jesus wants His church to be a disciple-making body."[39]

# SET S.M.A.R.T. GOALS

One of the best ways a leader can prepare for a glocalized vision, is to always be very *specific* when it comes to planning out their dream. For example, if you say, "I want to go on a mission trip," that's not specific. But if you say, "I want to go on a mission trip to Lebanon, next summer, for at least one week," that's specific. Everything you do must be specified not only for your own organizational needs, but for clarity throughout your team. Being specific is the first point in a five-point strategy I use to keep myself and my team on track. It's called the S.M.A.R.T. approach to planning, explaining, and pursuing any goal.

This S.M.A.R.T. acronym first appeared in the 1981 paper, "There's a S.M.A.R.T. Way to Write Management's Goals and Objectives," by George T. Doran, a consultant and former Director of Corporate Planning for Washington Water Power Company. According to Doran, the odds of reaching a goal were greatly increased using the S.M.A.R.T. strategy:

**S**PECIFIC: Have a definable target to pursue/improve.
**M**EASURABLE: Be able to measure forward progress.
**A**TTAINABLE: Choose a goal that is within the realm of possibility.[40]
**R**EALISTIC: Expect realistic results that are achievable using available resources.
**T**IMELY: Specify exactly when results can most likely be realized.

As you can see, the second point is having a *measurable* goal. Making sure you have a measurable goal guarantees: a) that you always have a goal in sight; and b) that you always have a way of determining if you're being successful or unsuccessful. For instance, if you set a goal to share the gospel with twelve people in one year, that is measurable, as opposed to simply declaring, "Next year I want to share the gospel." You must be able to measure your goal. Numbers, of course, are the most straightforward way to keep a goal measurable (e.g., making one disciple, going on three missions, writing six articles). What's important to remember is to always set your quantity based on reality: specifically, the skills you possess, the resources at your disposable, and most importantly, the guidance you are receiving from God.

This leads directly to *attainable*, which relates to setting a goal within the realm of possibility. This isn't to say that God will not do the impossible for us if we are faithfully following His will. What I mean is that we shouldn't set a goal that is so far outside the realm of logic, reason, and faith that it borders on absurdity. For instance, if I were going on a missionary trip to China in one month, I might set a goal of speaking Chinese fluently, in thirty days, for a missionary trip to Beijing. That, however, isn't a S.M.A.R.T. goal. It's specific. It's measurable. But it's simply not attainable. I might as well say I want to fly in thirty days. A truly S.M.A.R.T. goal would be to learn perhaps 10–20 key phrases in Chinese before going on the mission.

Closely linked to attainable is the *realistic* point. In whatever situation you may find yourself, you must make sure your goal is realistic. If it's not realistic, you'll end up wasting a lot of your time, talents, and treasure. And you'll likely end up rather depressed and discouraged. I've seen this lead to so much frustration and disappointment that some people have simply thrown up their hands, saying, "I give up. I can't do it. God isn't blessing me. I'm not called." But the truth is that they had set unattainable and unrealistic goals at the outset.

Finally, a goal must be *timely*. There must be a time-limit set for achieving the goal. Otherwise, any number of distractions—other projects, new obstacles, or even just fatigue—can keep pushing the goal farther and farther away into the future. And this isn't something limited to ministry. Even in our ordinary lives, when it comes to anything that needs to be accomplished (at home *or* at work), it's always best to have a time-line/time-limit.

A great example of a goal that we can test would be a common goal set by many Christians: reading the Bible. Suppose a person were to think to themselves, *I'm going to read the whole Bible in one week*. Let's see if that is a S.M.A.R.T. goal:

| | |
|---|---|
| Is it **S**pecific? | YES (reading the whole Bible). |
| Is it **M**easurable? | YES (sixty-six books). |
| Is it **A**ttainable? | YES (anyone is capable of reading the entire Bible). |
| Is it **R**ealistic? | NO. Very few people could read the Bible in a week, even if they were to spend all of their waking hours reading! This doesn't even take into account the amount of time a person must devote to family, friends, work, and relaxation. |
| Is it **T**imely? | YES (one week). |

As you can see, a goal can meet as many as four out of the five S.M.A.R.T. points, but still not be a good idea.

## HAVE GOD'S HEART

Perhaps the most important aspect of having a glocalized vision is embedded in our understanding of God's heart, which is what helps us realize it's our Christian *duty* to spread the gospel to all nations (Matt. 28:19). Remember, the Bible doesn't say God sent His Son because he loved Jerusalem. It says, "For this is how God loved *the world*: He gave his one and only Son, so that everyone who believes in him will not perish but have eternal life" (John 3:16). And Acts 13:47 tells us, "'I have made you a light to the Gentiles, to bring salvation to the farthest corners of the earth.'" Even in the Old Testament, for those who looked forward to the gospel, the Psalmist wrote: "Give thanks to the Lord and proclaim his greatness. Let the whole world know what he has done" (Ps. 105:1).

It all boils down to obeying the Great Commission; we must be faithful to the last command Jesus gave. Christ's Great Commission to us was the climax of all His teachings, the culmination of thirty-three years on Earth and three years in ministry. And it fits perfectly into our whole section here on being connected with like-minded believers because only together can we succeed at having a church-wide glocalized vision. This is the very essence of what Christ's church is all about. As the prophet Isaiah declared: "'Thank the Lord! Praise his name! Tell the nations what he has done. Let them know how mighty he is!'" (Is. 12:4).

For some people it's not easy to have a glocalized vision because that's not what they were taught early in life. Psychologists tell us that what we learn in our formative years basically sets up how we, as adults, perceive ourselves and the world around us. Sadly, this often leads to us building walls in our heart and mind against perspectives that run contrary to what is familiar. This is a major problem because as sinners we have a variety of perspectives that aren't godly. So, it's up to us to start seeing things God's way, especially when it comes to ministry. We must focus our sights through God's spiritual lenses. How does *He* see people? What does *He* want for people? If you take such a perspective, you'll eventually get a glocalized vision.

This is what my good friend, Brian Satterlee, did in order to receive a glocalized vision that merged perfectly with the work of Levant Ministries. Brian is an extraordinary man of God who has authored numerous books on Strategic Management, Knowledge Management, E-Commerce, and International Business. He's also worked in the construction industry, been a small business entrepreneur, and has served as a consultant to various government agencies. He's even held the position of dean at three universities.

I first met Brian when I was his student at Liberty University, where he was a business professor. He had a great walk with God and was heavily involved in various ministries. But he didn't have a heart for the Middle East. This was understandable. Arabic-speakers were a group of people far removed from anything he'd ever known. But once I shared my story with him, he made a connection to Arabic-speaking people through my struggles. After graduating, I stayed in touch with Brian, and several years later shared with him my dream of Levant Ministries. In fact, I asked him to be the ministry's Chairman of the Board. And he said, "Yes." It was a miracle!

What changed Brian? It was just my personal story. In my testimony he saw a young man who loved God and who loved God's people. Then, as he went beyond himself by opening up his mind and heart, God blessed him with a far-reaching glocalized vision. He started thinking: *We have brothers and sisters in the Middle East who need our help, prayers, and support; they are potential converts who need to hear the Gospel.* Now, he's not only Chairman of the Board for Levant, but he's one of my closest friends, counselors, and advisors. He was actually one of my very first supporters! But if you had asked him before we met whether he'd ever be involved in a ministry to people in the Middle East, he likely would have answered, "What for? What does that have to do with me?" Sometimes a glocalized vision can arise simply through one person sharing their heart, dream, and story with another person.

Of course, all of this will mean nothing if we don't possess a willingness to step out of our comfort zone. Even I had to do this as I prayed about what my dream might be. You, as a NextGen leader, must go into the world and open your eyes to see what God is doing in the global community. Go on a mission trip! Why not? From what I've seen, the missionaries who are sent tend to be changed more than the ones they were sent to change. On a mission, they're able to see God, His power, and His work in totally new and fresh ways.

## REMEMBER THAT LOVE IS THE ANSWER

It's quite apparent that God wants us to be active locally, as well as globally. But what about the "love" aspect of the church's global call to spread the gospel? To be blunt, without the "love" part of this *glocalized vision*, we might as well give up. First Corinthians 13:1–13 (one of the most famous Bible chapters) makes it clear that although we "speak all the languages of earth and of angels," if we don't "love others," we're only a "noisy gong or a clanging cymbal."

Love must be the force that drives, strengthens, and guides us, especially if our dream is difficult. Levant Ministries, for instance, sends teams to some of the darkest and most dangerous places in the world such as Syria and Iraq. Only love could sustain us. Levant Ministries would break apart if those involved in our outreaches were not motivated by love, which according to scripture, is a core attribute of God's divine nature. "God is love" (1 John 4:8). It's no wonder that scripture repeatedly and resoundingly declares God's love and how it must be inextricably woven into the very fabric of our Christian identity.

Without God's love motivating us, we're hardly different than humanitarians. These individuals certainly do a lot of admirable work, but they're not interested in changing people for eternity. Like humanitarians, Christians should be feeding the poor, helping to educate the illiterate, caring for the sick, and fighting for human rights. But the *ultimate* goal for believers is to meet the *spiritual* needs of people around the globe by introducing them to the Savior. This is our motivation—people are either going to be eternally *with* God or eternally *without* God.

If you're driven by a glocalized vision of love, God will make a way for you to succeed as you pursue your dream. He will bless your activities because that's where God's heart resides (e.g., with the lost, the broken-hearted, the spiritually sick, the poor in spirit, the prisoners of sin). Pursuing any dream will only be truly successful if you look at the world through God's eyes, using His spiritual point of view. Every problem in the world must be combatted, first and foremost, with Christ's love. This is the only way to achieve lasting/eternal victory, not only for others, but also for yourself and those about whom you care. Everything affects everyone these days, no matter where you may be located in our world. As Queen Rania Al-Abdullah of Jordan has observed: "We look at problems happening halfway across the world and we think, 'Well, that's their problem.' But it's not. When you solve somebody else's problem, you're solving a problem for yourself because our world today is so interconnected."[41]

Here is the bottom line: If you want to be part of what God's doing, you must be active locally *and* engaged globally. You need to be a local leader with a global perspective. You must make the effort to take yourself on a journey around the world, either literally or via technology, to see what God is doing on a global scale. He's saving people, healing people, bringing people back to life in Christ. God is working right now, even in the midst of horrible suffering and widespread uncertainty about the future.

We have no idea what God might be up to. For example, what if the present tragedies involving refugees from Syria, Iraq, and other Middle Eastern countries is something God is using to bring people to Christ? Amal's story is a great example. Remember: "God causes everything to work together for the good of those who love God and are called according to his purpose for them" (Rom. 8:28). I've often wondered about this possibility while watching the pain of my Middle Eastern brothers and sisters over the last several years. And one thing that's struck me is how most of the Iraqi believers I've met in the U.S. and Europe accepted Christ as their Savior after the Gulf War, once they immigrated to Jordan, or after the 2003 Iraq War, when many of them went to Lebanon.

As this clearly shows, no matter what's happening, in the midst of *any* chaos, we must keep God's perspective and maintain our focus on what He's doing, believing that our Lord is in control. History is unfolding before our eyes, and we can choose to just be spectators, or, we can choose to join God's team in order to change the world for Christ.

---

**4**

---

# GO DEEPER WITH GOD

Until you know God as He is, you'll never become all that He's created you to be.

— Chip Ingram —
Living on the Edge[42]

**D**uring my senior year at Liberty University, I decided to spend one hour every day communing with God at a quaint little place on campus called Worley Chapel. It wasn't fancy or modern. It was simple and intimate. I wanted to meet God as I'd never met Him before. So, I made my vow. Despite my many projects, I was going to spend an hour with God, every day.

It was an easy appointment to keep, until one night after I'd been working in the computer lab for end-on-end hours that stretched long into the night. In fact, I was still working at midnight, even as the security guards were locking down doors and closing up gates. But I had to remain. Several deadlines were fast approaching and I still had a lot of work to complete. Finally, at around 2 a.m., I simply had to leave. I was too exhausted to stay any longer. So, I stumbled out to my car, got inside, and headed toward my apartment off campus. My eyes were barely open. My body was racked with fatigue. All I could think about was my bed, which I could almost hear calling my name from far away. Sleep was going to feel so good.

Then, suddenly, I realized I hadn't gone to Worley Chapel for my one hour with God. "Noooo," I thought. "Oh, no." I faced a decision: *God or Bed? God or Bed? God or Bed?*

I eventually made a U-turn and headed back to campus. And when I arrived at the gate, the security guard said, "Hey, why are you coming here so late? It's 2 o'clock in the morning."

I sheepishly replied, "Well, I just left the computer lab. I was there all evening. But I need to get back on campus now . . . uhm . . . so I can go to the chapel."

He looked at me a suspiciously, then laughed. "Ahhhh, go home son! You can pray at home. It's late."

"No, no, no," I answered, trying to make him understand. "I need to go *to the chapel to meet with God.*"

He must have thought I was nuts. And it took more than a little convincing on my part for him to let me through. But he finally allowed me on campus to meet with God for that one hour. Unbelievably, when I came out of the chapel a little after 3 a.m., I actually felt empowered, refreshed, energized, and ready to take on the world! God had been there waiting for me.

I look back now on that night, so thankful that I followed through with the promise I'd made to my Lord. This is what leaders do. They keep their word— not to earn something, not to prove something—but because a servant of God simply keeps their word, to God, first, and to people, second. If you want to be a NextGen leader, keeping your word is one of most basic characteristics you must cultivate. As the rest of this chapter will show, there are several other qualities that every potential leader should be strengthening and solidifying.

## LIVE LIKE A CHRISTIAN

Before anyone becomes a NextGen leader, or even before anyone starts seeking a God-given dream, one foundational pre-requisite must be met: they must be a true, dedicated, and maturing follower of Jesus. Then, only after someone knows Christ, can a walk of true *spirituality* begin. Every Christian, especially a leader, should be living a life of *true spirituality*. Mere "religion" gets you nowhere and does nothing. Plenty of "religious" people are around. But God wants persons living out *true spirituality*, which is the only way to know God (in an ever-maturing way) and to make God known (in an ever-expanding way). A *deep* relationship with God is what I'm talking about, not something that's superficial, immature, or complacent.

My dear friend and close mentor, Pastor Chip Ingram (CEO and Teaching Pastor at Living on the Edge), who wrote one of the best books on this subject, *True Spirituality*, insightfully identifies Romans 12:1–21 as the premier chapter of biblical guidance to experiencing true spirituality. According to Pastor Chip, Paul's letter presents five points:

- **Surrendered to God** guides you to giving "God what he wants the most" (Rom. 12:1);
- **Separate From the World's Values** enables you to "get God's best for your life" (Rom. 12:2);
- **Sober In Self-Assessment** compels you to "come to grips with the real you" (Rom. 12:3–8);

- **Serving In Love** frees you to "experience authentic community" (Rom. 12:9–13);
- **Supernaturally Responding to Evil With Good** helps you to "overcome the evil aimed at you" (Rom. 12:14–21).[43]

Chip explains: "What God really wants is not your religious performance. . . . He wants you to offer all that you are and all that you have to Him. He wants your heart, lock, stock and barrel."[44] Herein lies the difference between *a religion about God* and a *relationship with God*. The former focuses on obedience to outward do's and don'ts that impart a sense of self-righteousness and earned salvation; the latter focuses on an ever-deepening union between us and God via a daily transformation of the self from being unlike Christ to being Christ-like.

Anyone not engaged in a truly spiritual life risks having a passive relationship with God that will stagnate. And there's always something waiting to hinder you: career, family, friends, school, and even ministry. Remember Martha and Mary? These women were friends of Jesus, as was their brother, Lazarus, whom Jesus resurrected (John 11:38–44). In Luke 10:38–42, we see Christ at their home, where His followers had come to hear Him teach. Mary, according to the story, "sat at the Lord's feet listening to what he taught." Martha, however, chose to stay busy—too busy to listen to our Lord. Then, when she complained to Jesus about her sister, He replied, "My dear Martha, you are worried and upset over all these details! There is only one thing worth being concerned about. Mary has discovered it, and it will not be taken away from her."

We can so easily fall into this same trap by believing we must be busy, busy, busy in order to get things done for God, all while ignoring our first priority, which is to be listening to His words of life. Christian activist and author,

Christine Cain (whom I mentioned in Chapter Two), addressed this very issue in her brief article, "Perspective of Purpose," saying: "We can miss so much of God and His greater plans and purposes because we focus on the unimportant, insignificant things that just happen to be screaming the loudest for our attention. Instead of focusing on the bigger picture and prioritizing what we are faced with, we often times get side-tracked and distracted by the immediate, seemingly urgent elements of life, rather than the things that are actually important and will have an eternal impact."[45]

I couldn't agree more. We can endlessly keep ourselves running around, doing all kinds of things "for God," but miss the simplest of crucial tasks: staying close to Him; hearing Him teach us; experiencing His presence. Each of these things are necessary for anyone who wants to be a NextGen leader. We must daily nurture a deeper understanding of God. This is the only path of true spirituality that leads directly to Christian leadership.

## KEEP HIS WORD IN YOUR HEART

I've known many people, including Christians, who own all types of Bibles: Red Letter, Interlinear, Parallel, Annotated, Chain Reference, Comparison Study, and Devotional. Yet they never use them. They might read a few verses now and then, usually at Christmas or Easter, but during the rest of the year these Bibles just sit on the shelf gathering dust. It's tragic. Scripture contains not only the very words of God (2 Kings 17:13; 1 Thess. 2:13; 2 Tim. 3:16–17), but also everything for us that pertains to godly living (Ps. 119:105; Prov. 6:23; 2 Peter 1:3).

And unlike other writings, God's Word is actually "alive and powerful" through the working of the Holy Spirit upon our hearts as we read it (Heb. 4:12). Have you ever read a verse that spoke to you in a unique way, about a very specific issue in your life? It made you think: *Wow! I get it! So, that's what that verse means. I never thought of it that way and it deals exactly with what I'm going through right now. Thanks, God. I needed that.* Then, perhaps years later, you read that same verse, but it speaks to you in a totally different way, about a totally different situation, at a totally different time in your life, with a totally different lesson! *That* is God. His holy words are alive and active, speaking to your soul through the work of the Holy Spirit.

The living quality of God's Word (Acts 7:38) raises an interesting issue that relates to what our relationship should be to the Bible. You heard me right: *relationship*. On this point, some fascinating observations were made in a 2012 *Relevant* article by Christopher Abel, the Young Adult Pastor for the United Methodist Church of the Resurrection:

> When it comes to knowing a living person, it can take years, if not a lifetime, to truly know and understand someone. . . . And while the idea of approaching the Bible as a living thing might seem like a strange concept, there is something sacred available to us when we give the scriptures room to be alive. When we encounter beautiful passages, we can love them back—knowing that God is in them and speaking through them. When we wrestle with dark or confusing texts, we can let ourselves feel uncomfortable, yet still trusting. When we encounter hope, we can celebrate along our scriptures. When we read of acts of justice, we can be inspired to imitate our book. When the words pour forth mourning and lamentation, we can sit alongside of them and offer comfort. When we read those red letters, the words of Jesus, we can feel gratitude to our pages for holding such sacred gifts from our Lord. . . . like most living things, it wants deeply to be known. When you read God's Word, what is taking place is more than just a one-way "study" from person to object. Instead, God's

Word is indeed living as God moves it to work in your life—and make you more like Him.[46]

Given the nature of scripture, we can rest assured that interacting with it will always bring blessings of some kind, either to: a) draw us into a deeper relationship with God; or b) glorify God. "'The rain and snow come down from the heavens and stay on the ground to water the earth. They cause the grain to grow, producing seed for the farmer and bread for the hungry. It is the same with my word. I send it out, and it always produces fruit. It will accomplish all I want it to, and it will prosper everywhere I send it'" (Is. 55:10–11).

The importance of scripture has been well-stated by The Gideons in the Introduction to each Bible they've placed in every hotel room in America:

> The Bible contains the mind of God, the state of man, the way of salvation, the doom of sinners, and the happiness of believers. Its doctrines are holy, its precepts are binding, its histories are true, and its decisions are immutable. . . It contains light to direct you, food to support you, and comfort to cheer you. It is the traveler's map, the pilgrim's staff, the pilot's compass, the soldier's sword and the Christian's charter. . . . Christ is its grand subject, our good its design, and the glory of God its end. It should fill the memory, rule the heart and guide the feet. . . . It is a mine of wealth, a paradise of glory, and a river of pleasure.

Is this the kind of book anyone should pass up? I think not. Our Lord has given us the "infallible declaration of His mind," said A.W. Tozer (1918–1963), the renowned pastor/preacher. Within the pages of scripture we have the "instructions of the Lord" (Ps. 19:7), the "word of life" (Phil. 2:16), the "sword of the Spirit" (Eph. 6:17), the "message about Christ" (Col. 3:16), and God's unvarnished "truth" (John 17:17). It is our very source of faith (Rom. 10:17).

## INCREASE YOUR FAITH

We often read in scripture about the power of faith—*not* faith in ourselves (and not faith in our faith, as some falsely teach), but rather, faith in our God. None other than Jesus himself taught that when great faith is present, great things happen (Matt. 21:21). In fact, after Jesus healed the blind man, the Lord told him, "your faith has healed you" (Mark 10:52). This man knew that Jesus was the Great Physician. He had *faith* that Jesus could heal him, even though that seemed impossible. Unwavering faith in God makes impossible things suddenly seem not-so-impossible. Faith gives us the temerity to move forward in the face of overwhelming odds.

George Mueller (1805–1898) was a man of faith, who remains one of the clearest examples of what it means to nurture a deeper walk with God. His path to ministry started at the age of twenty-one, when he came to God and renounced his drinking, gambling, and even, thieving ways. He was about as distant from Jesus as anyone could get. It took him years of growth and training to get to a place where God could use him. But finally, in 1829, he received his first pastorship. Then, in 1830, he took his first real leap of faith by refusing a salary. Mueller feared that taking a salary might compel churchgoers to give financially out of "duty rather than desire. . . . [H]e only accepted voluntary gifts from those that wanted to support him."[47]

Mueller's trek of faith continued, culminating in his incredibly bold dream of opening orphanages for the abandoned children of the streets. This might not sound like a big dream today, but in 1835 it was utterly impossible. A cholera epidemic was raging in his area of England. He had no modern means of communication through which to request funds. He had no social, political, or cultural clout. He didn't even have a building. And he had no money.

Yet he pushed on, opening his first pseudo-orphanage in April 1836 by re-arranging his own rented home. Six months later, he opened a second house nearby. A third was opened in 1837, and a fourth in 1845. Then, in 1847, Mueller bought a parcel of land for £10,000, which he received after he prayed for a miracle. Not only did he get the money needed, but he purchased the land for below market rate. The land owner—Mr. Benjamin Perry—had a dream the night before meeting Mueller, a dream in which he saw Mueller asking for the land. Perry told Mueller that he believed God was instructing him to sell the land for orphans at a less-than-market rate.[48]

Each year Mueller expanded his dream to include more orphanages for children of all ages, boys and girls, from places far and near. By the end of his life, he'd cared for more than 10,000 children. (By way of comparison, in 1834 there were accommodations in *all of England* for only 3,600 orphans!) Even more unbelievable, Mueller never once directly asked for money. Yet he raised millions of dollars. Sometimes funds and/or supplies didn't even arrive until *literally* hours before needed. Solid faith, as Mueller's life shows, is an invaluable asset. "Faith shows the reality of what we hope for; it is the evidence of things we cannot see" (Heb. 11:1).

When it comes to faith, it's our job to simply do the *possible* by being conscientious, diligent, and responsible in our work. God is in charge of the *impossible*. As Mueller explained, "Faith does not operate in the realm of the possible. There is no glory for God in that which is humanly possible. Faith begins where man's power ends."[49] Mueller actually praised God's tests of his faith, saying, "The more I am in a position to be tried in faith, the more I will have the opportunity of seeing God's help and deliverance. Every fresh instance in which He helps and delivers me will increase my faith. The believer should not shrink from situations, positions, or circumstances in which his faith may be tried, but he should cheerfully embrace them as opportunities to see the hand of God stretched out in help and deliverance."[50]

## PRAY YOUR DREAMS

Prayer is one of the most direct routes to having a deeper walk with God. Sadly, one thing I've noticed in the ministerial world is that prayer is often relegated to a low level of importance. For example, during many business meetings and strategic planning sessions I've attended, prayer has usually gotten only a fraction of the time. Hours, and hours, and hours were spent talking, and talking, and talking. But only a minute or two was spent in prayer at the outset of each gathering. This is not the way it should be. All of us need to spend more time praying.

Prayer is our connection to God, as scripture promises, "The Lord hears his people when they call to him for help. He rescues them from all their troubles" (Ps. 34:17). Hebrews says, "So let us come boldly to the throne of our gracious God. There we will receive his mercy, and we will find grace to help us when we need it most" (Heb. 4:16). And Jesus instructed us to "always pray and not give up" (Luke 18:1).

George Mueller, as previously noted, was a man of great faith. But he also relied on deep communion with God. "I live in the spirit of prayer," he told others. "I pray as I walk about, when I lie down and when I rise up. And the answers are always coming."[51] The results were incredible. He received "fifty thousand specific recorded answers to prayers in his journals, thirty thousand of which he said were answered the same day or the same hour that he prayed them."[52]

Prayer might best be thought of as the vehicle in which our faith rises to God's presence, much like incense (Ps. 141:2). We take our prayers to God, having faith in His ability to grant our petitions for His glory. God responds, granting those petitions that will give Him glory, while simultaneously maximizing our spiritual growth. My friend, Hank Hanegraaff (Christian Research Institute), has outlined the F.A.C.T.S. of prayer that show not only the importance of prayer, but the right attitude to have toward this means of communicating with our Creator:

FAITH: "Faith is only as good as the object in which it is placed. . . . The secret is not in the phrases we utter but in coming to know ever more fully the One to whom we pray."

ADORATION: "Prayer without adoration is like a body without a soul. It is not only incomplete, but it just doesn't work. Through adoration we express our genuine, heartfelt love and longing for God."

CONFESSION: "The concept of confession carries the acknowledgment that we stand guilty before God's bar of justice. There's no place for self-righteousness before God. We can only develop intimacy with the Lord through prayer when we confess our need for forgiveness and contritely seek his pardon."

THANKSGIVING: "Failure to do so is the stuff of pagan babblings and carnal Christianity. Pagans, says Paul, know about God, but "they neither glorified him as God *nor gave thanks to him*" (Romans 1:21, emphasis added). . . . Carnal Christians likewise fail to thank God regularly for his many blessings.

They suffer from what might best be described as selective memories and live by their feelings rather than by faith."

**S**UPPLICATION: "[T]he purpose of supplication is not to pressure God into providing us with provisions and pleasures, but rather to conform us to his purposes. As we read in 1 John 5:14–15, "This is the confidence we have in approaching God: that if we ask anything according to his will, he hears us. And if we know that he hears us—whatever we ask—we know that we have what we have asked of him" (emphasis added).[53]

Interestingly, sometimes God doesn't choose to answer the most reasonable prayers, but instead, He chooses to answer the most outrageous prayers! "God honors bold prayers because bold prayers honor God," says Mark Batterson, pastor of National Community Church. "He loves it when we ask Him to do things we can't possibly do ourselves." Mark adds, "I believe that's the way God gets the glory."[54]

In Ephesians 3:14–19, Paul gets very specific, outlining the basic purposes of prayer, all of which serve to deepen our walk with God. In the Lifeway article, "Prayer: Your Power Connections, Dr. Phil Briggs (professor emeritus at Southwestern Baptist Theological Seminary), lists these purposes: "To derive the riches of the Heavenly Father. To gain strength in your inner being and receive God's power for living. To open your heart to God's presence. To be grounded in God's love. To understand the many dimensions of God's love. To express thanksgiving and praise to God. To confess sin and express dependence upon God for grace and forgiveness. To petition God for needs."[55] Dr. Briggs adds, "The Scripture is clear with many directives for us to pray. Jesus told the apostles a parable on the need to "always pray and not give up" (Luke 18:1).

And speaking of Jesus, even He had to pray (Matt. 14:23; Mark 1:35;

John 11:41–42; Luke 5:16, 11:1, 22:43–44, Matt. 26:36–44). The great stalwart of Christianity, R.A. Torrey, noted that Jesus prayed in "the early morning . . . . all night. . . . before all the great crises in his earthly life. . . . [after] great achievements and important crises. . . . when life was unusually busy. . . . before the great temptations of his life. . . . without ceasing. . . . and at all seasons."[56]

In light of Jesus' prayer life, it's fairly obvious that going deeper with God must include dedicated prayer time. First Thessalonians 5:17 goes so far as to say, "Never stop praying." You might think the verse is just God's use of hyperbole for effect. But this is one scripture that Pastor Bill Hybels has really taken to heart:

> Pray when you're alone. Pray when you're with a lot of people. Pray when you're in small groups. Pray on your way in; pray on your way out. Pray in your closet, in your car, at your desk. Pray morning prayers, pray mealtime prayers, pray in between mealtimes. Pray fervently, expectantly, and un-self-consciously. Pray when you're burdened, worried, sick, or brokenhearted. Pray when you're soaring, setting records, or dancing on a mountaintop. Pray when you're up, and pray when you're down. Pray when you're healthy, when you're sick, when you feel like it, and when you don't. (Especially when you don't.)[57]

In *Before Amen: The Power of Simple Prayer*, Christian author, Max Lucado, makes another great point: "Prayer is not a privilege for the pious, not the art of a chosen few. Prayer is simply a heartfelt conversation between God and his child."[58] This idea reflects Lucado's keen observation that if we look at all the prayers in scripture, each one can be distilled down to one basic prayer: "*Father, you are good. I need help. They need help. Thank you. In Jesus' name, amen.*"[59] It's so simple. Just. Talk. To. God. After all, we're His adopted kids, who are so close to Him and loved by Him that we can call Him Daddy (*Abba*, see Rom. 8:15 and Gal. 4:6). "So, let us come boldly to the throne of our gracious God. There we will receive his mercy, and we will find grace to help us when we need it most" (Heb. 4:16).

Lucado also admits, however, that praying can be difficult. His own struggles are common to all of us: "I doze off when I pray. My thoughts zig, then zag, then zig again. Distractions swarm like gnats on a summer night. . . . I think of a thousand things I need to do. I forget the one thing I set out to do: pray."[60] Moreover, it often seems impossible to carve out from our busy schedules even just a few moments to speak with God. Then, if we at least get that far, we fail to follow through with our plan. We miss days, skip weeks, sometimes go MIA for months! But you can't allow such a thing to happen if you're going to build a dream team. Prayer is your direct access line to God as you seek to make decisions and overcome difficulties.

Fortunately, we're not alone: "[T]he Holy Spirit helps us in our weakness. For example, we don't know what God wants us to pray for. But the Holy Spirit prays for us with groanings that cannot be expressed in words. And the Father who knows all hearts knows what the Spirit is saying, for the Spirit pleads for us believers in harmony with God's own will" (Rom. 8:26–27).

To summarize, then, every Christian must be praying continually. Every moment of every day should be bathed in prayer. Why? First, because God told us to do it. Isn't that alone a good enough reason to pray? Second, because we need it. It's a crazy world out there (and only seems to be getting crazier). Prayer keeps us rooted and grounded in Him. Third, and most relevant to our discussion, prayer is a must because it's through prayer that God teaches us, shapes us, sharpens us, and matures us in preparation for whatever ministry awaits us.

## DO AS I DO

Another hallmark of a life that is committed to God and on course toward a deeper Christian walk involves one's actions. Do you walk the walk (not just talk the talk)? "'Some people have faith; others have good deeds.' But I say, 'How can you show me your faith if you don't have good deeds? I will show you my faith by my good deeds'" (James 2:18). Prior to this striking comment, the apostle explained: "Suppose you see a brother or sister who has no food or clothing, and you say, 'Good-bye and have a good day; stay warm and eat well'—but then you don't give that person any food or clothing. What good does that do? So you see, faith by itself isn't enough. Unless it produces good deeds, it is dead and useless" (vv. 15–17).

I can't stress enough the importance of living out your faith through godly actions and spiritual activities. It's only by your outward deeds (i.e., good works) that the world can see your inward faith. My late mentor, Pastor Jadd Boulos, lived every day with this truth uppermost in his mind. He told me that he'd ask the Lord each morning to send to him someone he could help so he could demonstrate his internal faith in an external way. Then, after praying, he'd actually spend the day looking for an opportunity to bless someone. How amazing is that?

I've incorporated this same prayer into my own life. Several years ago I began praying, "Lord, send me someone today who I can encourage. Send me someone to bless. Bring someone into my life to whom I can give my time, talent, or treasure." Much to my surprise, when I started praying that prayer, the Lord began opening many doors of opportunity. He also brought all kinds of blessings to me; the kind of blessings money can't buy. This practice moved my focus from the material world to the spiritual realm. And my life hasn't been the same.

This isn't to say that we should do good works to get something. No. We should do good works only to please God. That should be our motivation, especially since every good work we do was pre-arranged and orchestrated by God for His glory: "For we are God's masterpiece. He has created us anew in Christ Jesus, so we can do the good things He planned for us long ago" (Eph. 2:10). We also should never for a moment think that doing good works is somehow related to obtaining our salvation (Eph. 2:8–9). The eminent Dr. Ghassan Khalaf—professor of Biblical Studies at Lebanon's Arab Baptist Theological Seminary—explains:

> Salvation is not through our good works. But through the presence of Christ in us who does the work through us. I was crucified with Christ, so I shall not live any longer [Gal. 2:20]. But Christ who lives in me. Not the Law [Rom. 5:20]. Not temples [1 Cor. 3:16]. It's Christ. I have died. Christ will live in me. My manners reveal Christ in me. My spirituality reveals Christ in me. The power in my life reveals the Holy Spirit's presence in me.[61]

In other words, our life is over, along with everything we would have pursued if we were still living for ourselves. We're no longer supposed to be driven by our own self-fulfillment. We're to be aligned with God's heart—living, thinking, acting, responding as Christ. If we do that, God will open up the gates of heaven and send opportunities for ministry growth, successful outreaches, and widespread evangelism (i.e., opportunities to advance God's kingdom).

## GROW A CHRIST-LIKE CHARACTER

Going deeper with God essentially means increasing our Christ-like character. It means taking the relationship we have with our Lord and manifesting it daily through our life. We are to love like Christ, talk like Christ, think like Christ, respond, serve, teach, and live like Christ. Being like Him must become a lifestyle that becomes more natural to us as time passes. We, as Christians, unlike unbelievers, have two natures—our sinful nature that is a slave to sin and our redeemed nature that has been freed from sin (Rom. 6:6–7; Gal. 4:7). Going deeper with God means living more consistently within that second nature.

In other words, you must reach a point where you can't do anything else *but* live a God-honoring life. You can't respond to others in any other way *but* the way Christ would respond. In time, hopefully, this way of life becomes more effortless. To use a few analogies, think of a puppy, a sparrow, and an apple tree. A puppy doesn't have to think about how to respond to a bright play-toy, or a stick that is thrown, or a bowl of snacks, or a wide open field in which to run. A sparrow doesn't have to figure out how to tweet, fly, or hunt for worms. An apple tree doesn't have to concentrate on growing branches, keeping the seasons, or producing fruit! NO! In a similar way, we, too, should simply live like Christ, naturally responding to the world.

Cultivating a Christ-like character, of course, is not something we do in order to prove ourselves to God. It's not how we earn points with our Lord. All of our motivation for cultivating a Christ-like character should come: first, out of our love for God; and second, out of our love for our neighbor. This reflects the answer Jesus gave to "an expert in religious law" who had asked him to cite the greatest commandment. Our Lord answered, "'You must love the Lord your God with all your heart, all your soul, and all your mind.' This is the first and greatest commandment. A second is equally important: 'Love your neighbor as yourself.' The entire law and all the demands of the prophets are based on these two commandments" (Matt. 22:35–40).

It all comes down to a making a conscious and intentional decision to improve our inner character. This is what turns non-leaders into good leaders, then turns good leaders into great leaders. We must be people of integrity who do the right thing in whatever situation we find ourselves—in public and in private. All of us must strive to be the same person in front of everyone: family, friends, church leaders. Our behavior can't be determined by our company.

My friend, Joseph, for instance, was really put to a serious test of integrity. He was offered an amazing job with a high six-figure-a-year salary and all kinds of enviable perks. All he had to do was to compromise his doctrinal purity, forsaking what he knew scripture taught, in favor of an aberrant teaching. These potential employers wanted him to not only endorse, but also publicly preach, what has been termed the "Prosperity Gospel." More specifically, they requested him to ask people to give money to the ministry so that those people would in turn be blessed/healed by God, which they claimed would be guaranteed if listeners donated a lot of money.

But Joseph, although he certainly believed that God does heal and bless people, also understood that scripture says nothing about God's blessings/healings being linked to (or based on) money that is given to a church or ministry. This put Joseph in a position of having to choose between: a) living honestly, according to his beliefs; or b) selling himself out (and rejecting biblical soundness) for money. He chose wisely by turning down the offer, thereby staying true to himself and true to scripture. And that decision of integrity honored the Lord. Interestingly, after he turned down this lucrative offer, God still blessed him, eventually leading him to start his own ministry that is today reaching millions of people across the globe.

Another example I can share about living with integrity, which basically means doing the right thing, comes from my own life. Several years ago, in the midst of seeking funds for Levant Ministries projects, I received a phone call from some rather wealthy individuals.

> They said to me, "Fares, we have a big project."
> "That's great! What is it?" I asked excitedly.
> "Well, we have a very large fund for Christians living throughout the Middle East."
> I couldn't believe my ears! "Wow, that sounds awesome," I said. "How can I help?"
> "We need you to help us find Christians who are ready to leave the Middle East."

I began asking questions. And it soon became apparent to me that what these men were actually trying to do was expel Christians from the Middle East! I was stunned. As attractive as that offer was to me, there was no way I could be involved in such a project. My entire ministry is to support Christian brothers and sisters *in* the Middle East—not remove them. Of course, if they had been simply trying to help severely persecuted Christians escape harm/death, that would have been a different story. But that wasn't their plan. They just wanted to expel Christians. Like my friend, Joseph, I had a choice to make. Was this project worth my integrity? No.

## BE AN ENGINE OF CHANGE

Living a life marked by devotion to *true spirituality, God's Word, faith, prayer,* and *Christ-like character* will always lead to a deeper walk with God, which in time, will transform any believer into what I like to call an *engine of change.* We see a perfect example of an "engine of change" in the biblical character, Esther, a poor orphaned girl who, through God's favor, rose to be the Queen of Persia. And in so doing, she saved her people from certain destruction (Esther 8:1–17). It's been called one of the greatest stories of inspiration ever told.

Esther never gave up. She wanted to accomplish something great for God by becoming the Queen. So, it was to God that she kept looking. She *never* looked to herself. That would have had destroyed her. It would have completely discouraged her. In her own strength, with her own resources, she never could have become the Queen. She was: 1) an orphan; 2) a refugee (in Susa, Persia); 3) a Jew; 4) a woman; and 5) poor. She faced many challenges, personally and culturally (e.g., personal trauma, social isolation, widespread prejudice/racism, physical danger) just because of who she was. But she never succumbed to these limitations. She didn't sit around feeling sorry for herself. And she never blamed anyone for her circumstances. Many people in her situation would have been angry, resentful, and bitter. But not Esther. She accepted her shortcomings/ challenges as opportunities to become the Queen, which turned out to be a miracle that glorified God in a way that stands out in history like a shining star.

Esther didn't allow her limits to limit her! She grew beyond her limits. She viewed her situation as a perfect setup through which God could demonstrate His miraculous power to the world. She yielded herself to what *could be,* rather than settling for what *was.* With such an attitude, we, too, can not only make great strides with Christ, but become *engines of change* throughout the entire world. Like Esther, we must remain uncompromising, persevering, and unwavering in our faith. She changed the world around her against all odds. And here we are today, thousands of years later, still talking about her.

Today, there are similarly inspiring pillars of the faith, who like Esther, show amazing strength, courage, and perseverance in the midst of extreme adversity. The spiritual wisdom and emotional maturity they demonstrate is often extraordinary, even though some of them might still be very young. One such individual would be ten-year-old Myriam—an Iraqi Christian—who was forced to flee Qaraqoush, Iraq (near Mosul) when ISIS took control of the town in mid-2014.

Myriam and her family ended up in Irbil, Kurdistan, where she was interviewed by Essam Nagy, the presenter of "Why Is That?," a popular Christian TV program that airs on SAT-7 KIDS.[62] Myriam was found by SAT-7 after she had already spent four months in a refugee camp. Although still traumatized to some degree by her ordeal, Myriam appeared as poised, mature, and thoughtful as any adult.

"Thank God. God provides for us," she said after being introduced Nagy asked, "What do you mean, 'God provides for you?'"

"God loves us and wouldn't let ISIS kill us. . . God loves everyone."

"Do you also think God loves those who harmed you, or not?"

"He loves them. But he doesn't love Satan."

Nagy pressed her further, curious to know how Myriam's young mind and heart viewed the horrifying events surrounding her and the destruction of her people. "What are your feelings towards those who drove you out of your home and caused you hardship?"

The little girl answered without hesitation, as if only one answer could be given; an answer so clear and obvious: "I won't do anything to them. I will only ask God to forgive them."

"You can forgive them?"

"Yes."

But that's very hard," Nagy replied. "Or, is it easy to forgive those who made you suffer?"

"I won't kill them. Why kill them? I'm just sad they drove us out of our homes."

Nagy at this point changed the subject to lighter things, asking her about school, and in turn discovering that she loved school. She was a very good student, she said. And she missed her friends, especially her best friend, Sandra.

"We used to spend the whole day together. All day at school we were together," she explained. "Even though we didn't live close by, we loved each other a lot."

Nagy just listened.

"And if we wronged each other, we used to forgive each other. Sometimes we used to play and wrong each other. But we used to forgive one another. We used to love each other. Now, I only wish to see her [again]. She loves me a lot. And I love her, too. And I hope to see her one day. I hope we go back home. And she goes back home."

"I hope you go back to a home that's better than your first home," said Nagy.

Myriam smiled and looked skyward. "If God so wants. Not what we want, but God, because He knows."

Nagy asked, "Don't you sometimes feel sad? Do you feel as if Jesus has forsaken you?"

"No. Sometimes I cry because we left our home and Qaraquoush. But I'm not angry at God because we left Qaraquoush. I thank Him because He provided for us. Even if we are suffering here, He provided for us."

"Do you know that Jesus will never forsake you?" asked Nagy, moved by this young girl's faith.

"He will never forsake me," Myriam replied confidently. "If you're a true believer, He will never forsake you."[63]

Young Myriam, along with other believers who share her spiritual depth, are great examples to follow as we pursue our God-given dreams. Seeking to emulate their attitudes and perspectives would help any Christian move forward along the road toward becoming a leader. But this is not the only way to progress in our spiritual maturity. There is also something called emotional intelligence (EI), which is a quality that each of us must train and increase throughout our lives. This will be the subject of Chapter Five.

## 5

# UNLOCK THE HEART OF THE MATTER

Don't let's forget that the little emotions

are the great captains of our lives,

and that we obey them without knowing it.

— Vincent Van Gogh —


People will forget what you said,

people will forget what you did, but

people will never forget how you made them feel.

— Maya Angelou —

n 2004, while living in Michigan and looking for a job, I had been attending a church that was going to host a special guest from Lebanon, Pastor Ayman Kafrouny. He was particularly important to me because his ministry had helped me move forward in my spiritual journey. So, I volunteered to not only pick him up from the airport, but also shuttle him around town.

There was one problem, however. I didn't have a nice car—not nice at all— quite *un*-nice, to be completely honest. This was because I didn't have a lot of money (an understandable predicament since I wasn't even employed). After some thought, I decided to rent a brand new car. But I could only do that by putting the rental cost on a credit card, a risky decision, to be sure, given my unemployed state. Nevertheless, I wanted to give Ayman a comfortable experience as we traveled around the city. It also just seemed like the right thing to do.

My plan, fortunately, worked out quite well. I was able to drive Ayman to where he needed to go, including back and forth to church, while feeling completely relaxed about the car. I actually had a great time acting the part of a chauffeur. He, too, seemed to enjoy the time we spent together and I could tell he appreciated my efforts. I was blessed beyond words.

But not until after I had dropped him back off at the airport for his departure did I discover how blessed I really was, extra blessed because he had left me a thank you note. And in that note was the *entire* financial offering the church had collected for him. It was his gift to me! I was stunned. The funds not only covered the car rental, but went beyond that amount.

Afterward, I realized how easily I could have missed this blessing. But by allowing myself to bless someone else, God could bless me. Don't misunderstand me. I'm not saying we should only *give* things to others to *get* things from God. My point is that we must be intentional about our actions/choices. Right actions that bless others don't just magically happen. They require a conscious act of one's will. Such choices take effort, clear-headedness, and resolve. And, as is so often the case, God will orchestrate specific situations that allow for those choices so we can see how far we've gone in our walk with Him, and we can see what level of maturity we've reached. A very big part of gaining spiritual insight is the subject of this chapter: *Emotional Intelligence.*

## DISCOVER EMOTIONAL INTELLIGENCE

As I mentioned in Chapter Four, spiritual growth is *the* requirement for any leader wanting to be successful. It all begins, obviously, with receiving Jesus as one's personal Lord and Savior (Rom. 10:9). Next, one must begin a journey of *true spirituality* marked by: ongoing biblical study, increasing faith, regular prayer, godly living, and the development of a Christ-like character. These attributes, as I also explained, will ultimately make you an engine of change in the world. But one additional aspect of a "true spirituality" journey is *Emotional Intelligence* (EI), which undergirds every other mark of maturity on the road toward being a leader. In fact, without constant growth in the area of EI, spiritual progression will almost be impossible.

EI is most commonly defined as "the ability to identify and manage your own emotions and the emotions of others" and generally includes three skills: 1) "emotional awareness;" 2) "the ability to harness emotions and apply them to tasks like thinking and problem solving;" and 3) "the ability to manage emotions, which includes regulating your own emotions and cheering up or calming down other people."[64] This is far different than one's IQ (Intelligence Quotient), which is a "number representing a person's reasoning ability (measured using problem-solving tests) as compared to the statistical norm or average for their age, taken as 100."[65]

An extraordinarily poignant (and highly entertaining) illustration of EI contrasted with IQ was noted in a 2013 *Psychology Today* article by Susan Krauss Whitbourne, Ph.D. (professor of Psychological and Brain Sciences at the University of Massachusetts Amherst and the author of sixteen books, including *The Search for Fulfillment*). According to Whitbourne, the lovable character Forrest Gump "provides the best fictional example, at least, of someone whose test scores placed him well below average in intelligence, but whose enjoyment of life—and success—were unquestionably high."[66] Gump, despite having a terrifically low IQ of 75, excelled in life by the sheer power of his indefatigable spirit, unyielding courage, and indomitable positivity that always seemed to place him in the right spot at the right time.

Such attributes, completely divorced from intelligence, are routinely present in those who succeed, whether they be athletes, artists, CEOs, soldiers, politicians, legal experts, physicians, entrepreneurs, religious leaders, or homemakers. As British psychologist Graham Jones has pointed out, "performance involves knowing how to use the skills you have, not just having those skills. It's no use to have a brilliant intellect if you can't work within the constraints of your environment or be motivated to use your brilliance to the max."[67]

The theory of EI was popularized in our modern era by psychologists Peter Salovay, (president, Yale University), David Caruso (research affiliate, Yale Center for Emotional Intelligence), and John D. Mayer (Professor of Psychology, University of New Hampshire), who created the Mayer-Salovey-Caruso Emotional Intelligence Test. In his 2009 article "What Emotional Intelligence Is and Is Not," Mayer explains what they discovered:

> People with high EI, we believed, could solve a variety of emotion-related problems accurately and quickly. High EI people, for example, can accurately perceive emotions in faces. Such individuals also know how to use emotional episodes in their lives to promote specific types of thinking. They know, for example, that sadness promotes analytical thought and so they may prefer to analyze things when they are in a sad mood (given the choice). High EI people also understand the meanings that emotions convey: They know that angry people can be dangerous, that happiness means that someone wants to join with others, and that some sad people may prefer to be alone. High EI people also know how to manage their own and others' emotions.[68]

Interestingly, positive traits that EI *doesn't* include are: agreeableness, optimism, assertiveness, happiness, calm, ambition, or any kind of get-up-and-go characteristic that enables someone to accomplish a task. These are mere qualities of an individual's personality. EI is much more specific—i.e., it is "the perception and cognitive integration of emotions."[69] In other words, EI is our ability to work productively with emotional data we receive from our internal and our external worlds, positively integrating both reason and logic with our emotions.

If EI sounds a little tough to fully comprehend, don't worry, you're not alone. Scientists, psychologists, counselors, and social workers have spent decades trying to concisely explain EI in a way that is as easily understood as IQ. But it's been difficult, to say the least. At this point, however, emotional intelligence has finally been broken down into four basic skills "that pair up under two primary competencies: *personal competence* and *social competence.*" Together these competencies control how well we "manage behavior, navigate social complexities, and make personal decisions that achieve positive results."[70]

| PERSONAL COMPETENCE | SOCIAL COMPETENCE |
|---|---|
| self-awareness (emotions) / self-management (behavior) focused on one's own responses to external stimuli, deals with internal conflicts | social-awareness / relationship-management focused on the moods, behavior, motives of others, deals with external problems |
| anger frustration sadness irritation | arguments negativity criticisms disorganization |

Given the significance of EI, no one is surprised that in the business world it has surpassed IQ in importance. Corporate executives/managers have discovered that high levels of knowledge and/or extensive experience means precious little if one doesn't have the EI to productively wield that knowledge/experience.

As *Business Insider* remarked, "Emotional intelligence can mean the difference between behaving in a socially acceptable way and being considered to be way out of line."[71] No leader, of course, wants to be out of line. And no leader wants those being led to be out of line. (This would hold true in any business, church, or ministry.) Widespread development of EI could effectively neutralize all kinds of problems in various organizations. *The Harvard Business Review* has gone so far as to describe EI as "a ground-breaking, paradigm-shattering idea that is one of the most influential business ideas of the decade."[72]

EI makes everything go much smoother since it's "essentially the way you perceive, understand, express, and manage emotions. . . . the more you understand these aspects of yourself, the better your mental health and social behavior will be."[73] This is why several companies, such as TalentSmart (used by 75% of Fortune 500 companies), now provide EI-oriented assessment tools, coaching procedures, and training programs for businesses. According to TalentSmart research, "emotional intelligence is the foundation for a host of critical skills."[74]

The excitement surrounding EI is understandable. Unlike pure intellect, emotional intelligence touches every facet of our being. And the benefits of achieving advancement in this area are almost incalculable. A well-developed EI can remove needless guilt, counter negativity, help resolve conflicts, assist in problem-solving, and provide encouragement in discouraging times. Not everyone, however, has a high EI. But hope is not lost. EI can be developed.

Of course, you don't decide today to be emotionally intelligent, and then tomorrow simply break all of your bad habits. It's a process— a lifelong process.

## EXAMINE YOUR SELF: PERSONAL COMPETENCE

The concept of emotional intelligence dates as far back as the famous Greek Oracle, at the Temple of Apollo, in the city of Delphi (c. 600–500 B.C.). There, inscribed in the forecourt, were the words "KNOW THYSELF." This reminded onlookers that knowing one's emotional motivations was a key to unlocking self-understanding. The second maxim prominently inscribed at the temple read: "NOTHING TO EXCESS" (i.e., "EVERYTHING IN MODERATION"). This reminded visitors to never forget that anything taken to an extreme was an emotionally undisciplined course of behavior that could easily lead to problems. Both of these concepts are addressed throughout scripture in a variety of ways.

The first aphorism is echoed in numerous verses that talk about reflecting on our actions, testing our motivations, looking at our behavior, and examining our beliefs/doctrines (Ps. 119:59; Lam. 3:40; Hag. 1:5–7; Rom. 12:3; Gal. 6:4; 1 Cor. 11:28; 2 Cor. 13:5). Given so many passages on introspection, it's understandable that many leaders regularly take breaks from their hectic lives to look inward and seek God. Bestselling author, John Piper, for instance, an American Calvinist Baptist pastor and the chancellor of Bethlehem College and Seminary, explained his inward journey in an enlightening 2013 *Christianity Today* article titled "Pastor, Know Thyself":

> No preaching. No book-writing. No blogging. No tweeting. No church responsibilities. I called it a soul check. With the help of my wife, Noël, and a counselor, I did more soul-searching than I can remember ever doing before. I wanted to know my most intransigent sins. And I wanted to make war on them in fresh ways.[75]

The second aphorism mirrors a number of biblical passages that contrast moderation with excess, and show the differences between them. This is actually a common theme in scripture. Consider King Solomon, who deliberately lived a life of excess just to experience it. "Anything I wanted, I would take," he confessed. "I denied myself no pleasure" (Eccl. 2:10). Ultimately, he learned that such pursuits are meaningless/empty. Excessive indulgence simply can't satisfy the human heart because what the human heart actually craves is God (v. 11). This is a heavy lesson that receives even more weight when taken with other verses indicating that anything taken to excess can be harmful/wrong: sleep (Prov. 6:9–11), alcohol (Eph. 5:18), church worship/teaching (1 Cor. 14:26–40), and/or work (see our need for the Sabbath, Ex. 20:8–10). Moderation is the key to self-control, which should rule all our actions (Prov. 16:32; Rom. 14:22–23; 1 Cor. 9:27).

EI also relates to how well we understand the various passions, attitudes, viewpoints, and thoughts that drive us to either: a) take certain actions; or b) speak certain thoughts. Again, scripture has a lot to say about these sides to our personality/character (1 Cor. 15:58; 2 Cor. 9:7; Col. 3:23; James 4:1–17). We must take time to examine and learn about ourselves if we're going to mature in Christ and find success in ministry.

Daniel Goleman, author of *Emotional Intelligence: Why It Can Matter More Than IQ*, explains, "If your emotional abilities aren't in hand, if you don't have self-awareness, if you are not able to manage your distressing emotions, if you can't have empathy and have effective relationships, then no matter how smart you are, you are not going to get very far."[76] Similarly, scripture says that "A person without self-control is like a city with broken-down walls" (Prov. 25:28). Think for a moment about Galatians 5:22–23. It's basically a mini-dissertation on EI: "[T]he Holy Spirit produces this kind of fruit in our lives: love, joy, peace, patience, kindness, goodness, faithfulness, gentleness, and self-control."

Self-control is not only commanded by God, but is an indispensable part of EI. It can sometimes be difficult, of course. And for some people, it's particularly difficult (due to personality, past experiences, or emotional wounds). But being able to keep a tight grip on your actions (Prov. 20:11; Phil. 1:27) and your speech (Prov. 21:23; James 1:26) is imperative if you want to be a leader. No Christian, especially a leader, can be like an unmanned vehicle careening downhill without breaks. But exactly how can self-control be increased?

I believe that maintaining/increasing self-control comes down to living by the biblical principles of righteousness that God has imparted through his Word. This is the key. So many people—sometimes even Christians—live unguided by spiritual/biblical principles. Yet situations often arise wherein we're given a clear choice to either live by God's principles or live by other principles from another source (e.g., society/culture, our sinful self, the views of others). Most difficult are situations wherein we're forced to choose between doing the right thing or doing that which will benefit us in some way (physically, financially, or even emotionally).

There can be no compromise with truth. Consider Daniel. He was guided by principles that demonstrated his worship of the one true God (Dan. 2:28 and 3:16-18). Despite all the physical comforts offered by the king, he held himself in check, choosing to eat minimal amounts of food. He controlled his appetites and desires, choosing to remain true to eating as God had commanded (Dan. 1:12). He was guided by the Lord. Before his hands moved to reach for something God had forbidden, he stopped himself. He put the brakes on his hands, so to speak, by first putting the brakes on his heart. This shows the basics of self-control—i.e., the ability to place either a hold, or a complete stop, on what your heart would normally/naturally want.

God has instructed us to look into our hearts so we can a) accurately assess our emotions, being ever-aware of them; b) live a life of moderation; and c) discipline our behavior (i.e., have self-control). This is exactly what secular leaders also seek to do. But there's a big difference when it comes to the "how" of it all. Unlike unbelievers, Christians have additional help in the form of the Holy Spirit, who assists us in delving deeper (i.e., deeper than our deceptive/ sinful minds). Proverbs 3:5 tells us "Trust in the Lord with all your heart; do not depend on your own understanding." This is crucial because, as the prophet Jeremiah taught: "The human heart is the most deceitful of all things, and desperately wicked" (Jer. 17:9).

Only God knows what is truly in your heart. So, the very first step toward EI for you, as a Christian, is to take a deep look at who you are *in Christ*. When you realize that you've been redeemed by God, that you're a new creation in Christ, that Christ gave you a new life, and that the past has gone—this is the primary reality you must inhabit each day. Your road, as a believer, began when you were born again into newness of life. You're no longer chained to the dark despair of the past, but are always looking forward to the bright hope of the future (Phil. 3:13). That alone will bring you closer to a higher level of emotional intelligence.

Then, as you advance, you'll gradually be able to more accurately and purposefully look at your strengths/weaknesses as God reveals your true "self." You'll begin seeing your emotions more realistically, and by doing so, arrive at a place where your emotions can be controlled and channeled. This is essential for any leader, but is particularly important for a Christian leader because a Christian leader represents God, as evidenced by the "man of God" title of honor (Moses, Deut. 33:1; Elijah, 1 Kings 17:18, Elisha, 2 Kings 4:7; David, Neh. 12:24). Every believer is an ambassador of Christ (2 Cor. 5:20).

As a leader, you simply *must* be able to assess your attitudes/perceptions, which will govern your actions, pursuits, responses, and decisions. Unfortunately, we sometimes have a tough time seeing our weaknesses/shortcomings. That's when God helps us by providing other windows through which we can gaze into our souls—e.g., trusted friends and loving family members. They often give invaluable insights into our attitudes, emotions, behaviors, decisions/choices. "Wounds from a sincere friend are better than many kisses from an enemy" (Prov. 27:6).

Remember, too, that Christ faced this same kind of temptation in the wilderness against Satan, after He'd fasted for forty days and nights (Matt. 4:1–2). He was at His weakest point! Satan cleverly tried at first to tempt Him using food as bait (v. 3). But Jesus responded with scripture (v. 4). Then, Satan taunted our Lord using a false scenario that pitted fear against faith (v. 5–6). Yet again, He replied with scripture, remaining in total control (v. 7). Finally, the Adversary sought to trap Jesus with perhaps the greatest weakness of humanity: pride (v. 8–9). At this final temptation, Jesus not only used scripture, but rebuked the Devil and cast him away (v. 10-11). Like Jesus, we can't cut corners. We must be fully controlled by the Holy Spirit (Rom. 8:14; Eph. 5:18; Gal. 5:18) and base our responses on the Holy Word of God (Ps. 1:1–6).

## RELATE TO OTHERS: SOCIAL COMPETENCE

In *How Successful People Lead*, John C. Maxwell outlines five different levels through which people pass as they go from being new/good leader to being a seasoned/great leader: *Position, Permission, Production, People Development*, and *The Pinnacle*. The first level is where people follow you because they must follow you. At the second level people follow you because they want to follow you. Once you reach the third level, people follow you because of what you've done for the organization you've been leading. Then comes the fourth level, where people follow you because of what you've done for them personally. Finally, there is the fifth level, at which people follow you because of who you are and what you represent.[77]

*Level-1* leaders are not true leaders. They're mere bosses. They give orders and people must obey. They don't lead a team. They command subordinates. They have authority that is used within certain boundaries, but no further. Such so-called "leaders" are only in their position because they were put there by someone else. They didn't necessarily earn it, nor do they need to be particularly well-suited with talents/abilities (*How Successful...*, p. 7).

*Level-2* leaders are leaders due to the most basic of reasons: they're liked. And they're liked because they've usually been kind, thoughtful, accepting, and trustworthy. They lead in a way that creates a positive environment wherein people genuinely have a good time following. A leader at this level has gone beyond their mere appointment. They've begun to connect with the people being led. They care about them as individuals, rather than focus on them as task-performers. In some ways, more than anything else, this level is a sort of getting-to-know-you level. It's a relationship-building phase marked by back-

and-forth communication that builds trust between the leader and those being led (*How Successful...*, pp. 7–8).

*Level-3* leaders are leaders who, by use of their skills, are really starting to get things done. Here's where a leader begins to truly shine by making things happen in the organization. By getting results, a leader at this level also starts building not just credibility, but perhaps more importantly, influence. "Many positive things begin happening when leaders get to Level 3. Work gets done, morale improves, profits go up, turnover goes down, and goals are achieved. . . . [L]eaders can become change agents. . . . They can take their people to another level of effectiveness" (*How Successful...*, p. 8).

*Level-4* leaders are truly great leaders, "not because of their power but because of their ability to empower others." It is here that leaders begin developing/training others to start walking the path toward leadership. Level-4 leaders, in a sense, reproduce themselves. They're now followed because of what is being done for those being led. Everything has become personal, rather than simply corporate. Lives are being changed. It's a level marked by great teamwork and a high level of productivity. But perhaps the most rewarding aspect of this level is how the relationships formed here "are often lifelong" (*How Successful...*, p. 9).

*Level-5* leaders display the ultimate in leadership skills and productivity. It's a journey that takes many years. Reaching this level "requires not only effort, skill, and intentionality, but also a high level of talent." The results are often extraordinary: e.g., the creation of other highly proficient leaders, the establishment of top-of-the-line organizations, the garnering of a sterling personal reputation, and the solidification of a lasting legacy (*How Successful...*, pp. 9–10).

I've cited these five levels because transitioning through each of them is how one matures in the *Social Competence* area of emotional intelligence. This is the other side to EI that's just as imperative as the *Personal Competence* side. It involves learning about others and being able to deal with their emotions (or EI). Here the goal is not only to get along with others (and respond appropriately to them), but to help others also grow if they're lacking in any area.

Our ability to focus on others connects directly to how well we can: 1) understand them; and 2) empathize with them. Being able to do both results in better relationships at work, school, church, and home. I used the term "focus" because the way to heighten our EI toward others is primarily through the attention we pay to those around us. We must train ourselves to be perceptive to changes in voice tone, body language, eye movements, and verbiage used. A lot can be known about someone's emotional state if we'll simply pay attention to them.

This Social Competence factor breaks down into two parts: "*Social Awareness. . . * your ability to accurately pick up on emotions in other people and understand what's really going on. *Relationship Management. . .* your ability to use awareness of your emotions and the others' emotions to manage interactions successfully."[78] These attributes of EI can be trained daily:

1. **Think about your reactions** — "People who lack emotional intelligence are more likely to just react, without giving themselves the time to weigh up the pros and cons of a situation and really thinking things through."

2. **See situations as a challenge** — Rather than stressing out over a conflict or controversy, look at it more like a puzzle to solve. Think of ways to possibly diffuse the situation (and try them), while identifying any ways that might exacerbate the issue (and avoid them).

3. **Modify your emotions** — When dealing with others, pinpoint what's causing you stress and change your focus to create a different emotion that will enable you to better deal with the other person. Also, try to pinpoint what's causing them to be stressed out, and seek to respond in a way that will calm their anxiety.

4. **Put yourself in other people's shoes** — This skill can be especially helpful in the customer service arena where irate customers tend to be rather abusive to those trying to help them. One of the best ways to use your EI during such a confrontation (or any volatile situation) is to imagine yourself as the other person. Consider what might be making them so angry, impatient, or frustrated.[79]

Notice that each of these exercises requires intentionality. You must make a deliberate choice of your will to respond/react in a way that will not add fuel to any fire. My point is illustrated well by a story I heard years ago about a woman in the drive-thru lane of a McDonald's. She was taking her time, unsure of what she wanted, ordering something, but then changing her mind; then, finishing her order, only to revise it by taking away a few items and adding others. Meanwhile, the driver in the car behind her was growing impatient and began venting his frustration by honking incessantly, yelling out the window, swearing, and making threatening motions. Finally, the woman finished and pulled up to make her payment, while the man behind her placed his order. She finally received her food and drove away. Then, when the man drove up to the pay window, much to his surprise, the woman had already paid for his meal.

Was she feeling guilty? Was she attempting to say, "I'm sorry for holding you up"? Was God prompting her to make this gesture to someone she had inconvenienced? We'll never know. But what we do know for certain is that her action was extremely intentional. It was a choice she made (for whatever reason). She needed to be in a certain state of mind to: a) think of such an act; and b) actually follow through with doing what she had thought of doing. It's with this level of intentionality that we must live each day, meet every situation, and deal with every person. That woman didn't give a knee-jerk response, but instead, thought through her choices; she chose not only using wisdom, but also godliness, compassion, kindness, and understanding.

This isn't something that comes easily or naturally. It's something we must constantly remind ourselves to do. It's a quality of our character that grows as we saturate our minds with God's Word and permeate our life with prayer. I call this mode of conduct self-generosity. It's when you can give unconditionally and have the ability to make sacrifices, not forcing yourself to do so, but doing so through a natural desire to live with a generous spirit.

## TIE IT ALL TOGETHER

EI is all about you knowing how to lead . . . *you*. Because *you* are the toughest person you will ever have to lead. And only after you learn how to lead *you*, will you really be ready to lead others. If you can develop this one skill, then you'll be well on your way to being an effective leader that God can use in a wide variety of circumstances under a myriad of conditions. I'm not pushing some kooky pop psychology. It's all biblical—Old Testament *and* New Testament.

In the Old Testament, we find countless passages dealing not only with self-awareness, but its corollary, self-control (i.e., self-management). Concerning self-awareness, the Psalms offer a plethora of passages on asking God for help in self-awareness. For example, Psalm 26:2 says, "Put me on trial, Lord, and cross-examine me. Test my motives and my heart." Occasionally, the Psalmist even speaks to himself in hopes of discerning what's going on with his emotions (see Psalms 42 and 43). And those who take time for such self-reflection are referred to as prudent (Prov. 14:8). Regarding self-control (or, self management), the Old Testament reveals, "Better to be patient than powerful; better to have self-control than to conquer a city" (Prov. 16:32; see also Prov. 25:28). Psalm 4:4 adds, "Don't sin by letting anger control you. Think about it overnight and remain silent." In other words, "Fools vent their anger, but the wise quietly hold it back" (Prov. 29:11). This applies to our speech, as well as to our actions (Prov. 13:3, 18:7, 21).

The Old Testament also addresses areas involving awareness of, and responses to, the emotions/thoughts of others. Proverbs 20:5, for instance, reads: "Though good advice lies deep within the heart, a person with understanding will draw it out." The point here is similar to the EI concept about one's need to handle others with understanding, and in so doing, being able to handle their emotions (and discern what's really going on in any given situation). Similarly, we find a variety of passages that deal with helping others (Prov. 3:27, 19:17, 22:9), resolving conflict/living peacefully (Prov. 12:20; Ps. 34:14), and passing righteous judgement (Lev. 19:15; Prov. 31:9).

Like the Old Testament, the New Testament repeatedly mentions self-awareness (Gal. 6:3) and self-control (1 Cor. 9:25; Titus 1:8). These keys to achieving EI are aptly summarized in Philippians 4:8–9: "Fix your thoughts on what is true, and honorable, and right, and pure, and lovely, and admirable. Think about things that are excellent and worthy of praise. Keep putting into practice all you learned and received from me—everything you heard from me and saw me doing. Then the God of peace will be with you." Romans 12:3 also sums up a developed EI: "Don't think you are better than you really are. Be honest in your evaluation of yourselves, measuring yourselves by the faith God has given us." We're plainly told that our thoughts must be renewed daily (Eph. 4:22–24) so that the attitude we possess is the attitude of Christ (Phil. 2:5).

Even Jesus indirectly taught EI from certain angles. In the area of Personal Competence, for example, He instructed His followers to look at their own hearts before leveling any condemnation or judgment: "'[W]hy worry about a speck in your friend's eye when you have a log in your own? How can you think of saying to your friend, 'Let me help you get rid of that speck in your eye,' when you can't see past the log in your own eye?'" (Matt. 7:3-4). Our Lord's conclusion echoes the need for EI reflection: "'Hypocrite! First get rid of the log in your own eye; then you will see well enough to deal with the speck in your friend's eye'" (v. 5).

Our Lord spoke even more plainly on Social Competence—i.e., awareness of the emotions being felt by others and how to appropriately respond to them, especially in tense situations. Consider the famous scene wherein Jesus was confronted with the adulteress and the people who wanted to stone her to death, according to the Law. He didn't condemn her, chastise her, or incite violence against her. Instead, He took time to assess her state of being (spiritual, mental, and emotional) and carefully analyzed the situation. Only then did he make his reply to the angry crowd, "'[L]et the one who has never sinned throw the first stone!'" (John 8:7). Social Competence can additionally be seen in His lessons on dealing with enemies (Matthew 5:38–40), treating others properly (Luke 6:31), and loving our neighbors (Mark 12:31).

Christ, of course, also exemplified EI for us in His own life by never losing control of His emotions, and never losing control of situations involving the emotions of others. He always responded with wisdom and insight permeated by love and compassion. This, despite the fact, that he was often verbally castigated. Some called him crazy (John 10:20). Others claimed he was a bastard (John 8:41). Some thought him to be a fraud and had no faith in him (Matt. 13:58). Many insinuated He was a blasphemous liar (Matt. 26:65). And a select few even accused Him of being demon possessed and in league with Satan (Matt. 9:34; Mark 3:22). And when none of these charges could be substantiated, Christ's enemies simply lied about Him (Luke 23:2), accusing Him of things He'd never taught or done. But Jesus always held his composure, even on the cross not reviling others, although He was being reviled. He went so far as to cry out, "Father, forgive them, for they don't know what they are doing" (Luke 23:34).

Such a perfect example of EI will always be out of our sinful reach. But in Christ we see the ideal to pursue. As Paul said, "I press on to reach the end of the race and receive the heavenly prize for which God, through Christ Jesus, is calling us" (Phil. 3:14). Or, as Hebrews puts it, "Let us. . . become mature in our understanding. Surely we don't need to start again with the fundamental importance of repenting from evil deeds and placing our faith in God" (Heb. 6:1).

—————— **6** ——————

# PAY FORWARD
# YOUR TREASURE

Moses had a stick. . . . David had a slingshot, and Paul had
a pen. Mother Teresa possessed a love for the poor; Billy Graham
a gift for preaching; and Joni Eareckson Tada, a disability. . . .
If you will assess what you have to offer in terms of your time,
your treasure, and your talents, you will have a better
understanding of how you might uniquely serve.

— Richard Stearns —
World Vision[80]

n Chapter Two, I briefly mentioned that time in my life when I thought God wanted me to be a worship leader. I was very young, in my early twenties, and I had just started out in ministry. I wanted to serve God. I wanted to glorify God. I wanted to please God. But I didn't know where, or how, to start. At that time, no one was willing to give me a venue, a pulpit, or a ministry. So, I started looking inward at my abilities and asked myself: *How much treasure is mine to give? Where can I offer my gifts/talents? What can I do with very little assistance?*

I soon thought, *Well, I like music. Maybe I can do that.* So, I wrote a few songs that I began sharing. And much to my surprise, people were blessed. They loved my songs! I then decided to invest even more of my time in the area of writing music, eventually producing a couple of albums after I'd graduated from college. I thought it would be financially impossible, but God moved in some of my friends' hearts to help me. The money just showed up when I needed it.

As time passed, more people began seeing that I could be a worship leader and bless the church through my music. They believed in me, prayed for me, encouraged me, and assisted me financially. They invested in me as I invested in my talents. This is one of the great things about moving in faith. When you trust God, He puts people in your path who will help move you forward. When I released my first CD, for instance, my church gave me a venue for a concert. And at that concert, thirteen people came to Christ. I was only 24-years-old and in awe of how God was using me. It was humbling. But that was only the beginning. God enabled me to produce more CDs, make countless connections with church leaders, and build a strong network with brothers and sisters who believed in my gifts. Eventually, my music went international!

Then, in 2013, as I started walking deeper with God and growing emotionally, as well as spiritually, I began seeing a bigger picture. I loved doing music. But that was just one talent of several talents God had given me. And my other gifts weren't being used at all. This sometimes happens. We focus on a single gift at the expense of other gifts that God might also want to use, gifts even more important and productive than the talent already being used.

I learned a valuable lesson: our talents must *complement* each other, not *exclude* each other. In my case, God used music to open up the world to me. He used it to introduce me to the church and to help me make connections that I would need for a greater purpose/mission. As I look back, I now see that everyone needed to get to know me first as a worship leader. Then, those connections/networks that I had created through music were able to help me when I founded Levant Ministries. The connections I made through my temporary music ministry enabled my lifelong evangelism ministry to succeed! Without those connections, Levant Ministries might have failed. But with those connections, Levant Ministry was able to quickly start developing leaders, sending out evangelism teams, creating original-content media, training thousands via our curricula, and helping other ministries to plant churches.

The temporary ministry thriving in the *present*, paved the way for the lifelong ministry of the *future*. And because of my experience in music, Levant Ministries was able to help other ministries create their own worship CDs. No aspect of the time, talent, and treasure that I had invested in music was wasted. God used everything. But none of it would have been possible if I had not been: a) committed to finding the treasure that God had placed in my heart; and b) open to paying it forward. These are two of the foundational building blocks of any lifelong ministry.

## LOCATE YOUR TREASURE

I recall how, when I first started out in ministry, I had a small vision. I had a limited understanding of what talents I possessed and how they could be used by God. I thought I might be able to, through God's grace, change the world by perhaps reaching tens of thousands via my music. But God's plan was bigger than anything I could have imagined. He wanted me to reach millions through Levant Ministries using varied projects, venues, and talents. Although music would not be *the* talent to take me to the end goal, it would be *a* talent to take me to the end goal.

This, of course, was *my* journey. It might not be *your* journey. Some people immediately discern their primary gifts, and in so doing, are able to instantly set off in a ministerial "lane" of operation, where they stay for years. But this is rare. It's more common for believers to go through some trial and error, as they seek to discover their treasure. And this *treasure hunt* always begins with someone simply offering up whatever they discern as their gifts in the present moment. In other words, focus first on one thing. Choosing one talent/gift to use when starting out is far better than taking a shotgun-approach (i.e., trying to do a million things at once). If you aspire to be a great leader of lasting impact, you must start using *today* whatever God has already given you, so that you can eventually discover whatever talent he might reveal *tomorrow*.

Concentrating on one task/talent at a time is also important because it can help you to not only better understand the gift you've already uncovered, but discover those gifts that remain hidden. There are no shortcuts. Some things just take time. And it takes time to test a talent after it's been activated. Just begin using whatever talent you possess in whatever way available to you. Then, see what God does. Watch how He blesses your efforts. Observe how others respond. Check your own heart to see how you're feeling about what you're doing.

Staying fixed on one thing at a time will actually make examining *every* area of your life much easier. It will bring clarity. Being unfocused, on the other hand, will have an opposite effect: confusion. This is a common pitfall for young people who, despite trying to find a direction, often find themselves muddled in their thoughts about themselves, others, and the world around them. They try many different routes to happiness, fulfillment and purpose, jumping from one school major to another, from one job to another, from one friendship to another, and from one relationship to another. This can be draining and distracting. You need to be more conscious of the "big picture" because as soon as you figure that out, things will look very different, especially when it comes to finally realizing your life's purpose/ministry.

Gradually, after a period of time, you'll start seeing whether or not a certain area of ministry is right for you. For example, if God is not really blessing your efforts in project coordination (e.g., if you're feeling spiritually, emotionally, and psychologically bogged down, or if others are not responding), then that particular talent might not be what God wants you to be doing as your main calling. Or, if the Lord is blessing you to a certain degree, even then, such a result might simply be a doorway to yet another gift/ talent you're meant to discover.

Don't forget: It takes time. *Slow and steady wins the race*, as Aesop's classic fable, "The Tortoise and The Hare," teaches. As is often said today, chillax. No need to panic. God is in control. As long as you're being sensitive to His promptings, everything will be fine. And if it's taking a while to find your gifts, don't think you're wasting time. Whatever you're doing—as long as you're doing it for God—will not be wasted. God will use your "starter-gift" in order to lead/ guide you, just like He used music (my "starter-gift") in my life (Rom. 8:28).

Also, make sure you talk to your circle of close friends, mentors, and spiritual leaders. During my early days of searching for my treasures, these individuals (persons who truly cared about me) offered their honest opinions about what they thought I possessed in the area of skills. They'd say, "Fares, you're effective in music ministry. But you might be able to be far more effective doing

_____." As I took their words to heart (and prayer), I started discovering different talents as an administrator, writer, speaker, and organizer. A whole new world opened up to me! And the results were amazing. Looking at ourselves through the eyes of others can be an extraordinarily revealing experience and can help us accelerate our discovery process.

## ACCEPT YOUR TREASURE

Everyone wants to achieve great things. But exactly how one goes from point A to point B is a challenge. Some people, sadly, spend decades seeking what they were designed/created to do, ignoring the obvious, in favor of some fantasy. This is tragic because God has given each one of us a wonderful set of *unique* talents and skills to use for Him. These gifts are a *personal* treasure. We were made "wonderfully complex" (Ps. 139:14) and implanted with skills God wants us to develop. It's part of a beautiful and perfect plan for each person (Jer. 29:11).

But far too many people look down on their treasure. This is why some individuals don't get very far in pursuing their dream. They don't believe that what they possess is good enough to succeed, or that their talents are sufficient to get them somewhere. So, they hide their talents, refusing to use them. Jesus addressed this in his parable of the "talents" (Matt. 25:14–30, NIV). In the New International Version, the Greek word commonly translated as "talents" is actually rendered more descriptively as "bags of gold" in order to better depict the word's meaning.

According to this parable, a rich man went on a journey. But before leaving, he entrusted his wealth to three servants. To the first, he gave five bags of gold. To the second, he gave two bags of gold. To the third, he gave one bag of gold. The first man put his bags of gold to work and gained five bags more. The second man also acted responsibly, and gained two more bags of gold.

The third man, however, simply dug a hole in the ground and hid his master's money in it. Eventually, the rich man returned and settled his accounts. To the first servant, and to the second servant, he declared, "'Well done, my good and faithful servant! You have been faithful in handling this small amount, so now I will give you many more responsibilities.'" But to the third servant, he said, "'You wicked and lazy servant! If you knew I harvested crops I didn't plant and gathered crops I didn't cultivate, why didn't you deposit my money in the bank? At least I could have gotten some interest on it.'" That servant's gold was then given to the first servant.

The lesson here is simple: *Use the gifts God has given you*. It doesn't matter *where* you start. What matters is *that* you start. Why? Because Matthew 25 tells us that God will only put us in charge of *big* things after we've been faithful in the *small* things. According to Francis Chan—former teaching pastor of Cornerstone Community Church and Founder/Chancellor of Eternity Bible College— there's no time like the present to start:

[T]here's a principle here: unless we're faithful with the little things, He's not going to entrust us with big things. In other words, people will say, you know, "I'll go overseas, I'll rescue kids, I'll do whatever." Okay great! But will you: work hard at your job?; will you study hard at your school?; will you be faithful to minister to the guy that's next to you in class?; will you talk to your next door neighbor?; will you start giving what God's called you to give while you're here?; will you stop watching so much television?; not spend so much time on the internet? Whatever it may be. And if we're not doing those little things, who are we to think God's going to entrust huge things to us. Because Jesus said, "That's not my pattern." He says, "If you're faithful in the little things, I'll put you in charge of big things." And He's talking about the things from Earth, in comparison to the things in heaven. . . . There's absolutely a principle here; that I got to watch the way I treat my kids, the way I treat my wife, and everything today. And do it diligently, faithfully. And then God will give me bigger things to do.[81]

Closely associated with this observation is another simple lesson from Matthew 25: *Don't hide your talents/gifts because you're either afraid, or embarrassed, to use those gifts for God!* I raise this point because some individuals, once they finally recognize the gifts that God has given to them, respond by coveting what He's given to someone else. This is a big problem. We must accept the gifts/skills God designed specifically for us, says Pastor Edward F. Markquart of Grace Lutheran Church, one of the largest churches on the West Coast:

> If you are jealous and envious of other people's giftedness or feel inferior, chances are you have not really accepted your own blend of gifts that God has given to you. One of the primary keys of life is to accept the gifts that God has uniquely given you, your unique blend of talents, aptitudes, abilities, life experiences, the sum total of all your resources. That means to accept the gifts you don't have, get on with life, and use the God given gifts that you have been given.[82]

Another struggle that plagues many Christians trying to use their gifts is failure. It happens. It's difficult. It hurts. But failure shouldn't cause you to feel embarrassed, disheartened, or apprehensive. Trial and error is actually part of many vocations and fields of study: science, teaching, medicine, and even politics. The key to success, to be honest, is not in always succeeding. It's in always being open to learning from your failures so that you can eventually have successes. *You must learn from your mistakes.*

John C. Maxwell—*New York Times* bestselling author, coach, and speaker—wrote a very helpful book, insightfully (and rather amusingly) titled *Sometimes You Win; Sometimes You Learn.* According to Maxwell, "A loss isn't really a loss if you learn something as a result of it. . . . You can choose to change, grow, and learn from your losses."[83] This sentiment was expressed well by Arianna Huffington, co-founder and editor-in-chief of the popular news website, *The Huffington Post*: "Failure is not the opposite of success, it's part of success."

Scripture bears out the truth of these remarks, repeatedly illustrating how the righteous may fail, but are never defeated by those failures. Consider Proverbs 24:16: "The godly may trip seven times, but they will get up again." The prophet, Jeremiah, wrote: "This is what the Lord says, 'When people fall down, don't they get up again? When they discover they're on the wrong road, don't they turn back?'" (Jer. 8:4). We *are* going to fail, either through ignorance, lack of skills, or sometimes even sin. It's a fact of life. But Psalm 37:23–24 assures us that the Lord "directs the steps of the godly. He delights in every detail of their lives. Though they stumble, they will never fall, for the Lord holds them by the hand."

Just try to keep in mind that a failure isn't truly a failure, if it's a failure while walking with the Lord. Failure is simply another tool in God's mighty hand that He uses to mold us, shape us, teach us, guide us, and instruct us. As a child of the Most High, despite our failings, we're able to boldly proclaim, "I have not achieved it, but I focus on this one thing: Forgetting the past and looking forward to what lies ahead, I press on to reach the end of the race and receive the heavenly prize for which God, through Christ Jesus, is calling us" (Phil. 3:13–14).

It's also important to remember what is actually the most amazing reason for why we sometimes fail: to glorify God! "We now have this light shining in our hearts, but we ourselves are like fragile clay jars containing this great treasure.

This makes it clear that our great power is from God, not from ourselves" (2 Cor. 4:7). This thought alone should be enough to help you accept your failures, even to be grateful for them, praising God for choosing to use you for His glory, despite your many imperfections, weaknesses, and yes, failures.

## INCREASE YOUR TREASURE

Once you've finally discovered the various talents God wants you to use for His Kingdom, and you've accepted them as yours to use for His glory, it doesn't mean you've finally arrived. You can't just sit back to enjoy a free ride. No. The talents, skills, and gifts you've received from God must be trained and used. Think of an athlete: a runner, a swimmer, a boxer. Although they may have innate skills, they must hone their skills with regular training and ongoing competition. This is exactly what every Christian must do, keeping a few things in mind.

First, you must be committed to using your talents, having a secure resolve in your heart that doing so is commanded by God. Rick Warren puts it like this:

> When God gives you a talent, he expects you to use it. It's like a muscle. If you use it, it will grow. If you don't, you'll lose it. If you have a talent but are afraid to use it, or if you get lazy and don't use it to benefit others, you're going to lose it. Like the parable of the ten talents in Luke 19, if you don't use what God has given you, he will take it away and give it to someone else who will. But if you use your talents wisely, God will give you more. If you use your time wisely, God will give you more time. If you use your energy wisely, God will give you more energy. If you use your influence wisely, God will increase your influence. God will bless your level of faithfulness.[84]

Second, you must place yourself (and your talents/skills) in the right environment—i.e., a good church. This links us back to Chapter One. A church is the #1 place God uses to grow us spiritually. We must be rooted and grounded firmly in a church, just as a plant needs to be: 1) firmly rooted and grounded in the right kind of soil; 2) surrounded by the right kind of climate; and 3) given the right kind of nutrients. If a plant is trying to thrive in the wrong environment, it's simply going to die. Nothing will be able to save it. So, too, will we (and our talents/skills) shrivel up and die if we're not in a good church (the right environment).

Third, you must connect with, and interact with, like-minded people who share the same kind of talents that you see emerging from within your own internal treasure chest. Take classes. Attend seminars. Go to conferences. Visit ministries. Seek mentors. Find role models. Get involved on a team pursuing a dream with which you can identify. Good connections can also be made through reading! A wealth of information exists in books, journals, and online articles that can educate you in countless subjects: missions, evangelism, apologetics, church planting, theology, _____ [fill in the blank]. All of these activities fall into the generalized realm of "personal development." (Cautionary note: remember that you're seeking spiritual growth to glorify God, not to just gain intellectual knowledge for the "self".)

Fourth, you must believe God will help you perfect your skills. God is ready and eager to help us in any/all endeavors that will glorify Him. This is the entire purpose of our life: *the glorification of our Creator* (Is. 43:7). As the Book of Revelation declares, "'You are worthy, O Lord our God, to receive glory and honor and power'" (Rev. 4:11: see also Ps. 86; Is. 60:21; Rom. 11:36; 1 Cor. 6:20, 10:31). One of the ways God is most glorified is by the use of our talents/ gifts. So, it only makes sense that He would grant us His help as we develop those talents/gifts. Psalm 84:11 promises, "The Lord will withhold no good thing from those who do what is right."

In specific reference to faith and its connection to our prayers/activities involving the growth of our treasure, Jesus promised, "'you can pray for anything, and if you believe that you've received it, it will be yours'" (Mark 11:24). Of course, this guarantee comes with a very important qualifier: whatever we ask for must *not* be desired for our own glory, nor should we ask for anything in order to just satisfy our sinful desires (see James 4:3). James made an incredibly revealing comment that is easily applicable to whatever trials and temptations we might face as we try to discover, accept, and increase our treasure:

> [W]hen troubles of any kind come your way, consider it an opportunity for great joy. For you know that when your faith is tested, your endurance has a chance to grow. So let it grow, for when your endurance is fully developed, you will be perfect and complete, needing nothing. If you need wisdom, ask our generous God, and he will give it to you (James 1:2-5).

Notice that it says "troubles of any kind." This is surely applicable to increasing one's skills/gifts/talents in preparation for a life of ministry and spiritual leadership. But rejoicing is still possible. Praise God! Why? Because God will always be present to strengthen, encourage, and help. Many of the greatest leaders in recent Christian history experienced extremely difficult trials on their road of growth/change that led to an increase in their treasure.

C.S. Lewis, one of the most renowned Christian thinkers of the twentieth century, had to mature through grief when his wife died. He could have fought against grief and turned against God. But he instead allowed his pain to mold him to the point of inspiration, using his experience to write *A Grief Observed*, a volume that ended up comforting millions of readers.

Corrie Ten Boom, the brave woman who helped hide Jews during WWII, had to fight through issues of forgiveness after she and her family were captured by the Nazis and taken to a terrible prison camp. She could have stopped growing/maturing by choosing to lock hatred in her heart and denying the gifts/talents God had given her. But she worked through her suffering, allowing God to shape her into a believer that reflected Christ brilliantly.

Consider, too, Joni Eareckson Tada, who at the age of seventeen, became paralyzed from the shoulders down. She, of course, had to courageously battle a number of emotional, psychological, spiritual, and physical issues. But she leaned on God. And through her commitment to the Lord, she not only *discovered* her talents, but also *accepted* her talents, and even *increased* her talents! She became: 1) an accomplished artist (using a pen/brush held in her mouth); 2) a bestselling author; 3) a notable public speaker; and 4) the founder of a worldwide, multi-million-dollar ministry (Joni and Friends) dedicated to helping the physically challenged.

Joni, Corrie, and C.S. all serve as shining examples of what it means for someone to receive from the Lord, then pay it forward.[85] This is what our life in Christ is all about! According to Chris Hodges, founder and senior pastor of Church of the Highlands, "Since the beginning of time, God has always wanted for people to know Him, find freedom, discover their purpose, *and make a difference.*"[86]

## PAY FORWARD YOUR TREASURE

Becoming a successful leader doesn't happen overnight. And achieving the spiritual maturity necessary to discover and utilize your treasure doesn't occur in a split-second. When you see someone excelling, you can know beyond a shadow of doubt that they've taken time to hone their skills with intentionality. They haven't found success by accident or chance. Major work was done via a conscious choice of the will in order to produce the results you see.

This kind of dedicated "work" in the area of spiritual maturity is actually not that different from the kind of dedicated work done in other areas of life. Take, for example, something as far away from spirituality as automobile manufacturing. To manufacture a safe, appealing, reliable, and useful vehicle requires thousands of nuts and bolts, hundreds of auto parts (some heavy, some light; some large, some small), and dozens of textured materials (rubber, glass, steel, plastic). To these materials, car makers must add all the time and labor needed to assemble the many pieces. Putting ourselves together as leaders entails the same kind of work. And I mean a *lot* of dedicated work: extensive research, ongoing study, and of course, a fair amount of trial and error. Through all of these activities, we assemble ourselves into the best leader we can be, and begin paying forward our treasure, usually by serving others: "God has given each of you a gift from his great variety of spiritual gifts. Use them well to serve one another" (1 Peter 4:10).

The very first place to start paying forward your talents would be in the local church, which allows your skills to be exercised in a community atmosphere. This is wise because it's within a tight community that you'll immediately start gaining valuable insights and making important observations. It's also within this community that your talents themselves will begin to evolve as they are used. Moreover, the church community is a place of safety, wherein you'll be given more freedom to fail, make changes, and fine-tune your skills. It's *the* place to make your initial (and likely largest) mistakes. There should be no place safer than your church family. It's unlike the world environment where, if you fail, there's not a lot of grace to be found.

Eventually, of course, the time will come for you to begin paying forward your treasure out in the "real world." This, at first, might be a little nerve-wracking. But just remember that with God by your side, giving you strength and support via the Holy Spirit, you can do all things through Christ Jesus (Phil. 4:13). It will also help if you regularly contemplate the possible effects you'll have not only in your church and local region, but throughout the world. Christians, as well as non-Christians, have changed the course of history by just paying forward their gifts.

The global importance of paying forward your unique treasure might best be illustrated in the story of one legendary American company led by a man who used his treasure to help save the entire world. The company was Ford. The man was Henry Ford. The time was 1941–1945. Even before the "Day of Infamy" (December 7, 1941), which launched America into WWII, Ford could feel the winds of war blowing toward the United States.

So, in the Spring of 1941, Ford began to construct the largest factory that had ever been housed under one roof: Willow Run in Ypsilanti, Michigan. "The goal: to build the U.S. Air Corps' biggest, fastest, most destructive heavy bomber at the time—the 56,000-pound B-24 Liberator—at an incredible rate of one-per-hour."[87] His foresight regarding the imminent need for planes was quite prescient. The figures released by President Roosevelt were staggering. To defeat Nazi Germany and the Imperial Japanese Army, the U.S. would need 60,000 planes, 45,000 tanks, and an appropriate compliment of ships, guns, and ammo.[88]

Fortunately, Ford's Willow Run factory was already in the fledging stages of operation when Pearl Harbor was bombed. In fact, the first piece of a B-24 was completed within two days of the attack. But there was still a lot to do before the plant could reach its goal of churning out one B-24 Bomber every hour of each 9-hour shift (400 planes every month). Ford used every talent, skill, and gift within his personal treasure trove to make good on his promise to deliver the planes. He made sure production increased month after month: "Willow Run produced 125 Liberators in September 1943, 150 in November, 165 in December, and 210 in January 1944. By November, Willow Run had birthed its first thousand bombers—and the second thousand were quickly on the way."[89] The pace continued: "In March [1944], Ford built 324 Liberators. April: 325. May: 350."[90] And by D-Day (June 6, 1944), Willow Run "came through on schedule with one four-engine Liberator an hour, 18 bombers a day, and by the end of the war a total of 8,800 big planes off the assembly lines and into the air."[91]

These planes were pivotal to the war's outcome, being one of the deciding factors that allowed the Allied Forces to defeat Hitler and Hirohito. The B-24 (and other aircraft, including the P-40 Warhawk, F4F Wildcat, P-51 Mustang, and F4U Corsair) gave America unquestioned air superiority. As General Dwight D. Eisenhower said, while he watched the planes flying overhead on the D-Day beaches: "If I didn't have air supremacy, I wouldn't be here."

This snapshot from history gives us but a small glimpse at the kind of influence that paying forward your treasure can have on the world around you. Ford literally helped change the course of history. Like Ford, you, too, can change the course of history. But unlike the story of Ford, which only focuses on a worldly battle, Christians are involved in a spiritual battle that can alter the future for millions of souls—saved and unsaved. It is a war of cosmic proportions with ramifications that can't even be calculated on an earthly scale: "For we are not fighting against flesh-and-blood enemies, but against evil rulers and authorities of the unseen world, against mighty powers in this dark world, and against evil spirits in the heavenly places" (Eph. 6:12).

One of my dearest friend, Nizar Shaheen, has fought this fight in an exemplary fashion. Our bond is quite special, not just personally, but also ministerially, since both Levant Ministries and Nizar's ministry (Light For All Nations) function in the same areas of the Middle East. We have literally traveled around the globe together and have seen thousands of people getting saved/baptized in numerous countries. He has for many years been one of my spiritual heroes. And my wife, Soha, actually gave her life to Christ during one of his evangelistic events in Gaza!

Nizar, who was raised in Cana of Galilee, was a rebellious boy whose mischief resulted in his being sent to a reform school in Jerusalem. Such a destination often solidifies a life of crime for many young boys in the Middle East, but in Nizar's case, it was the best thing that could have ever happened to him. That's because it was there that his journey with God began.

It all started when a priest arrived and called all the children together. He asked: "Who would like to serve the Lord when you grow up?"

For some reason, Nizar raised his hand. Perhaps he was curious. Maybe he was being mischievous. Or, he could have just been making a joke of some kind.

(To this day, he himself has no explanation for why he raised his hand.) Not surprisingly, all of the other kids laughed. They all knew what Nizar was like—how he acted, how he spoke, how he caused trouble. But for whatever reason, Nizar prayed, "Lord, when I grow up, I want to serve you." As the days passed, however, little changed in Nizar's life. And after five years he had forgotten all about the prayer.

But God didn't forget. He began calling Nizar years later, after he'd returned to Galilee. It happened one day when Nizar was working with his brothers as a stone mason. While building a mosque, Nizar fell from a high rooftop. He plunged head-first, flipped in mid-air, and landed hard on the dirt below. Everyone ran to Nizar, believing he'd been killed. But he was alive, which was no small miracle, given the height from which he'd tumbled.

He was immediately rushed to the hospital, and can still remember how, as he lay there unable to move in the back of the vehicle, he heard a voice. It wasn't an audible voice, but it was an inner voice—the loudest voice he'd ever heard. This voice, in Arabic, said, "Do not fear, for I have redeemed you. I've called you by your name. You are mine." He knew this was divine; he knew that God was trying to get his attention. But Nizar didn't fully grasp what it meant.

Even after he'd accepted Jesus as his savior, that day remained somewhat of a mystery to him. Only much later, after he began studying his Bible, did he discover the true meaning behind the message spoken by the "voice." It finally made sense when for the first time he read Isaiah 43:1: "'Do not be afraid, for I have ransomed you. I have called you by name; you are mine.'"

Nizar couldn't believe it. "I was amazed," he would later say. "This is what I had heard! This is the voice that I had heard from the Lord! And I was amazed that this was a verse in the Bible. An actual scripture! I thought it was only a voice from the Lord, or something divine. But in reality, it was a verse from the Word of God. Of course, that confirmed the calling of God. And the purpose of why God had called me." Neither Nizar, nor his life, would ever be the same:

> I knelt beside my bed and I said, "Lord, I know you have a divine purpose for my life. As I was dedicated to do evil (I was sold to do evil), now you can consider me sold 100% for your cause. I'm not only believing in you, but everything within me, in my being, every cell, every drop of blood, is going to be for your cause."[92]

It would be an understatement to say that Nizar has followed through with his promise. In 1984 he founded the first and longest-running Arabic language Christian TV program, *Light For All Nations*. Today it's one of the most popular Arabic language shows being broadcast in the Middle East. The production, which initially started in Toronto, now covers all of Canada, parts of the U.S., and the Middle East. It "is currently on four satellites, broadcasting four times daily, with a potential viewing audience of over 400 million people, covering all of North Africa, the Middle East, the Gulf countries, and much of Europe. *Light For All Nations* is also aired on some local and national stations, such as in Sudan, Lebanon, and Tanzania."[93]

Nizar's straightforward goal is to "reach the Arabic-speaking world, both children and adults, with the message of the Good News of Jesus Christ and to provide them with the opportunity to accept His gift of salvation."[94] To accomplish this goal, Nizar has used a variety of outreach tools for more than thirty years.[95] And his efforts have produced amazing results.

In mid-2017, for instance, Nizar traveled to Aleppo, Syria, where he led hundreds of lost souls to Jesus. This was an incredible achievement. Aleppo is rated the most dangerous city in the world. The once-thriving metropolis used to be home to five million residents, but since the Syrian War, has been reduced to a sprawling mass of bombed-out ruins that shelter barely a million terrified residents. More than 500,000 have been killed in Aleppo; more than two million have been wounded. And those who remain, live in fear every hour of every day, surviving on little food, with no electricity and no running water. Many are now blind. And even more have lost limbs.

But Nizar and his teams have worked tirelessly "to bring smiles on their faces and hope to their hearts."[96] According to Nizar, despite the hardships and horrors, the Body of Christ in Aleppo has remained "courageous and resilient." The pastors, he reports, have been ministering around the clock. "They are doing a wonderful job to show the love of Christ! They are providing generators to give electricity and have drilled deep wells to provide water for their community, whether they be Muslim or from a Christian background."[97]

Some of the stories are riveting. In one hospital, Nizar found a young man who lay badly injured from an artillery shell that went off next to him while he was in the city. He accepted Christ as his savior. A young woman, despite having her husband and small son killed during the warfare, still holds in her heart the peace and joy of Jesus. Another woman, a Christian for sixteen years, is known throughout the region as an incredible pillar of faith, one of the area's great soul-winners whose preaching for Jesus is unstoppable.

There are even stories of former terrorists who have become believers. One man, for example, a former member of the Muslim Brotherhood, was called by God just as he was about to massacre untold numbers of people using a suicide bomb vest. God spoke to him mere seconds before he committed this terrible act. "Why are you killing innocent people?" he heard a voice say. According to Nizar, "[f]ear seized him and he ran out, risking his life to cut the fuse leading to the dynamite before it exploded." Afterward, this young man started watching the TV show produced by *Light For All Nations* and "became a believer in Jesus Christ." Eventually, this young man had a son, whom he aptly named, Nizar.[98]

Like Nizar, you as a NextGen leader must diligently pursue the dream God is wanting to reveal to you, using the treasure He's already given you. The world is waiting. Evil is spreading across the globe. People are spiritually dying and living as slaves in spiritual darkness. So, the time is now to GO, GO, GO in fulfillment of the Great Commission (Matt. 28:16–20), as I discuss in my next chapter, "Think Locally, Act Globally."

## 7

# THINK LOCALLY, ACT GLOBALLY

As I see our world right now, I have never seen greater confusion, greater loss of meaning, greater uncertainty, and greater fear of what looms in front of us. Politics has gotten out of control everywhere. Nobody sees a mascot or a leader, and everyone wants to know what really lies ahead here. . . . The Gospel of Christ, as we speak to the masses, is multiplied opportunity of individual conquest. His message conquers the individual, and life changes.

— Ravi Zacharias —
Ravi Zacharias International Ministries[99]

I magine you're *not* sitting where you're actually sitting right now. Instead, you're shipwrecked on a deserted island, or lost in Africa, or stranded near the desolate Australian Outback. It's evening and you are safe. . . for the moment. But you've just drunk your last drop of water and you know the next day will bring blistering heat. You also know it won't take long to die of dehydration once the burning sun takes its place in the sky. The temperature will steadily rise from an uncomfortable 84° just after daybreak, to a sweltering 96° around late morning, to a merciless 110° by mid-afternoon. You will not survive. Fortunately, there's a watering hole full of water just ten feet from where you've stopped. Unfortunately, it's far from clean (thanks to a kangaroo family that just bathed in it). What do you do?

Well, if you have the know-how and the right supplies, you can just use the salt-enhanced version of the Solar Water Disinfection (SODIS) Emergency Method of disinfecting microbiologically-contaminated water. According to Brittney Dawney (Dept. of Civil Engineering, Queen's University) and Joshua

M. Pearce (Dept. of Materials Science & Engineering, Michigan Technological University), SODIS is "one of the most technically simple, affordable, and practical systems for disinfecting microbiologically-contaminated water."[100]

This process is about as easy as anything can be. You simply place water into some transparent plastic bottles and leave them in the sun for about six hours (or 48 hours in cloudy weather) "so heat and ultraviolet radiation can kill most pathogens. . . . Joshua Pearce found that SODIS can [even] be used on water that has been made murky by clay, but only after it is treated with table salt because salt causes the clay particles to stick together and settle out."[101] The process kills not only bacteria, but protozoan parasites and inactive assorted viruses. This solution is "being used by more than 5 million people in . . . African, Asian, and Latin American countries."[102]

The use of salt is particularly interesting. It acts as a binding agent that pulls out and settles the solid impurities, while the heat and ultraviolet light kills the harmful microbes invisible to the naked eye. In the end, the water is not only safe to drink (no microbes, parasites, or viruses), but palatable (no clay particles that would taste awful and probably gag you). "Pearce, who has drunk the salted-water, said that it has a lower sodium concentration than Gatorade and that he would use it 'no question' if he was somewhere with no clean water."[103]

## SHINE THE LIGHT, SPREAD THE SALT

I don't think it's coincidence that Jesus used salt and light to describe believers. "You are the salt of the earth" and "You are the light of the world" (Matt. 5:13–14). His message is plain: we, as Christians, are supposed to be agents of illumination and purification in the lives of those we touch, which in turn will change the world. Christ was using popular understandings about salt and light that have now been confirmed and further expanded during our modern era.

Both of these elements were viewed very highly in Christ's day, often being mentioned in literature and in cultural discussions as positive symbols. Light was indicative of goodness, divinity, righteousness, and enlightened understanding. Things done "in the light" signified truth, integrity, and a lack of shame (as opposed to things done "in the dark"). This is why ancient myths and legends regularly spoke about good "beings of light" fighting evil "creatures of darkness." Similar references can still be found in contemporary literature. Salt, too, was thought of as good (even divine) during the first century. It was valued not only for its preservative properties, but also for its ability to add flavor and zest to the most mundane of meals.

T.V. Philip—a lay member of the Mar Thoma Church, who has worked throughout India, Europe, USA and Australia—has rightly observed, "The Christian's task is to be the salt of society, preserving, reconciling, adding taste, giving meaning where there is no meaning, giving hope where there is no hope. It is about the quality of life." And regarding light, Philip has explained, "Christians are to be torch bearers in a dark world. . . . [W]e should shine so that others may see our good deeds and praise God; Shining does not mean self-propaganda, self-publicity, self-glorification, but bearing fruit in our life, bringing life and light to others."[104]

Today, all Christians, especially Christian leaders, must keep striving to be salt and light throughout the world. "Don't live like fools, but like those who are wise," wrote Paul. "Make the most of every opportunity in these evil days" (Eph. 5:15–16). In reference to Christ's teachings on the subject, evangelical author John Stott (1921–2011) expressed keen awareness of why we should live as salt and light: "Like salt in putrefying meat, Christians are to hinder social decay. Like light in the prevailing darkness, Christians are to illumine society and show it a better way."[105]

Living as salt/light is a basic responsibility of *all* Christians, but it's even more essential in the life of a leader. And considering the state of our world, being salt/light is needed now as never before. The world is engulfed in spiritual darkness and billions are dying of spiritual thirst. So, we must be lights, pointing the way to Jesus, who alone is *the* light of the world (John 8:12). And we must serve as salt, showing the way of righteousness in Christ, who alone is *the* source of pure living water (John 4:14, 7:38–39). Those who thirst for healing/deliverance and long for the light of salvation/forgiveness must be told the good news. *You are the light; you are the salt!*

## REALIZE THE DEPTH OF THE PROBLEM

For anyone who watches the nightly news, it isn't difficult to see that we're living in an era marked by enormous threats to our health and security. Humanity, in fact, is living neck-deep in an unprecedented state of global instability, chaos, and suffering.

### TERRORISM

When it comes to international terrorism, for example, the year 2015 saw "a 650% increase in fatal terror attacks on people living in the world's biggest economies [i.e., "the 34 countries that make up the Organization for Economic Cooperation and Development (OECD), which includes the US, UK, Germany, France, and Turkey]. . . . Five countries—Iraq, Nigeria, Afghanistan,

Syria and Pakistan—experienced the worst attacks, accounting for 72% of all deaths from terrorism in 2015. Syria saw a 50% rise in terrorism from 2014 to 2015."[106] The result? In 2015, a total of 29,375 people were murdered by terrorists throughout all countries worldwide. According to Steve Killelea of the Institute for Economics and Peace, "the continued intensification of terrorism in some countries and its spread to new ones is a cause for serious concern and underscores the fluid nature of modern terrorist activity."[107]

Tragically, Christians have often been the target of terrorists. And yet, even in the face of such horrors, somehow God is still glorified. I can't help but reflect here on the life and death of Abdelmassih Enwiya, a man from Aleppo, Syria. I learned of Abdelmassih from my good friend, Michael Chabo, a Syrian refugee who settled in Milwaukee, WI. He shared the story of Abdelmassih during our October 2015 NEXTGEN Conference. Michael's father was the pastor of the church in Aleppo, where Abdelmassih attended and served.

Little is known about Abdelmassih, but one of the things we do know about him is that at some point he began attending a Christian church, where he became a born-again believer. We also know he attended medical school, and after becoming a doctor, returned to his village in Northern Syria. There, he continued to grow in Christ, even having a mentor who would often visit him for prayer and spiritual support. His simple hope was to help the helpless. Tragically, the village in which Dr. Abdelmassih lived was invaded by ISIS. The terrorists eventually left, but they took 230 Syrian Christians with them, including Dr. Abdelmassih.

For many months no one heard a thing about their beloved physician, who was known throughout the whole region as a great servant of God and a very humble man. Then, ISIS began releasing videos featuring their prisoners.

And several of them showed Dr. Abdelmassih. Finally, ISIS released one last video—a shocking one that showed the executions of three Christians. One of the men in the video was Dr. Abdelmassih. He was calm. He was at peace. He knew the time of his death was near and he endured his final moments with silent resolution to the fate that had befallen him. But there would be more to the martyrdom of Dr. Abdelmassih.

According to those who knew what had happened during the seven months of his captivity, Dr. Abdelmassih was a tireless witness for Jesus. In the midst of his fear and anguish, he never stopped speaking to his captors and fellow captives about Jesus' love. In fact, he prevented many of the prisoners from renouncing their faith, assuring them of Christ's presence and encouraging them to hold fast to the truth. This is probably the reason why Dr. Abdelmassih was killed. He was essentially serving as a sort of pastor for those being held by ISIS.

As a final note to Dr. Abdelmassih's life, his last words, which to those who know Arabic, will forever be a poignant message. To understand Dr. Abdelmassih's message, one must understand that his name *Abdelmassih* literally means "a servant of Christ." What is significant is that throughout the various ISIS videos that included him, he had always introduced himself using his medical title—e.g., "My name is *Dr.* Abdelmassih" or "I am *Dr.* Abdelmassih." But in the last ISIS video, which showed him seconds before his brutal beheading, his last words into the camera were simply, "I am Abdelmassih." In other words, "I am a servant of Christ."

That was the end of his story on earth. But it was only the beginning of his story in heaven. Abdelmassih lives on, just as much "a servant of Christ" with God as he was with us. As one Syrian evangelical leader said in a tribute, "[Dr.

Abdelmassih] was a great man of God who took a risk by staying in his village to take care of his people and encourage them in the Lord."[108]

## POVERTY

Poverty is another source of alarm. According to the World Health Organization, poverty is "the world's biggest killer and the greatest cause of ill-health and suffering across the globe."[109] This contradicts one of the most widely held myths about poverty—that it only results in sub-standard housing, inadequate nutrition, and meager possessions. But the ramifications of poverty, especially extreme poverty, are much more devastating:

> Poverty is the main reason why babies are not vaccinated, why clean water and sanitation are not provided, why curative drugs and other treatments are unavailable and why mothers die in childbirth. It is the underlying cause of reduced life expectancy, handicap, disability and starvation. Poverty is a major contributor to mental illness, stress, suicide, family disintegration and substance abuse. Every year in the developing world 12.2 million children under 5 years die, most of them from causes which could be prevented for just a few US cents per child.[110]

The 2015 poverty statistics are staggering: "795 million people—or one in nine people in the world—do not have enough to eat. . . . Nearly half of all deaths of children under 5 are attributable to under-nutrition. . . . [translating to a] loss of about 3 million young lives a year. . . . Every 10 seconds, a child dies from hunger-related diseases. . . . About 896 million people in developing countries live on $1.90 a day or less. 22,000 children die each day due poverty. . . . 663 million people lack access to clean water. 2.4 billion people do not have adequate sanitation. Each day, nearly 1,000 children die due to preventable water and sanitation-related diarrheal diseases."[111]

## WAR

War, too, is an unavoidable topic. We not only continue to see several ongoing conflicts (e.g., Afghanistan, Syria, Iraq), but we now face the specter of yet another World War, possibly, a nuclear one involving the United States, China, Russia, and/or North Korea as the primary powers. Although tensions among these countries have been building for several years, 2016/2017 saw a marked increase in animosity, especially in relation to nuclear tests by North Korea. As a result, in January 2017, members of the *Bulletin of the Atomic Scientists'* Science and Security Board moved their "Doomsday Clock" to two and a half minutes to midnight.

The bulletin was started in 1947 by the scientists who helped develop the first atomic weapons possessed by the United States. Their symbolic doomsday clock "is widely viewed as an indicator of the world's vulnerability to disaster."[112] According to the 2017 *Bulletin*, "'[t]he probability of global catastrophe is very high, and the actions needed to reduce the risks of disaster must be taken very soon.' In 2017, we find the danger to be even greater, the need for action more urgent. It is two and a half minutes to midnight, the Clock is ticking, global danger looms. Wise public officials should act immediately, guiding humanity away from the brink."[113]

By way of comparison, the Doomsday Clock hasn't been this close to midnight since 1953, when the U.S. and U.S.S.R. began testing Hydrogen Bombs during their arms race.

## THE ENVIRONMENT

Finally, there is the environment, which presents an entirely different set of dangers that could potentially affect not only our current generation, but every future generation. At least three main environmental problems currently threaten the very existence of Earth as a planet that can sustain life: *pollution;* *deforestation;* and *soil degradation.*

First, we're facing increased *pollution,* especially carbon, which is produced primarily by the burning of coal, oil, gas, and wood. Reams of scientific data show it is causing various forms of climate disruption. This is bad news, very bad. "[C]limate change may be one of the greatest threats facing the planet. Recent years show increasing temperatures in various regions, and/or increasing extremities in weather patterns."[114] The effects have been, and will continue to be:

- more/stronger hurricanes;
- more/longer droughts;
- more frequent/intense "super storms,"
- cold weather in new regions (e.g., Europe);
- warm weather in new regions (e.g., the Arctic);
- a melting of polar ice, which has begun to change the delicate salt/fresh water balance of our oceans.

Unless pollution is decreased, the ongoing climate disruptions will at some point actually make Earth uninhabitable. All life will simply die due to the obliteration of our atmosphere.

The second environmental problem is *deforestation,* which is happening at an alarming rate: "Today, only about 30 percent of Earth's land mass is covered in trees. Each year, forests the size of Panama disappear. At the current rate, the world's rain forests will disappear within 100 years."[115] This is an issue because "[n]ot only do natural forests act as biodiversity reserves, they are also carbon sinks, keeping carbon out of the atmosphere and oceans."[116] In other words, forests keep the animal kingdom in balance, while at the same time the trees convert carbon dioxide into oxygen through photosynthesis, thus preserving our atmosphere. None of this might sound too important, but biodiversity and abundant foliage are both crucial to our survival.

Consider the simple honeybee. Bees may appear rather inconsequential (except to those who love honey), but if all honeybees died, we'd likely lose a majority of our food diversity. Bees, as most everyone knows, are the world's busiest pollinators. In fact, just about everything you eat on your plate at each meal has some kind of connection to the honeybee. So, "if a cataclysmic event sent all our bees into rapture [i.e., died], the aftershocks would ripple up the food chain. . . . [F]rom a diversity standpoint, things would be bleak. Much of our produce, like almonds, peaches, plums, apples and cherries, rely on bee-assisted pollination. In fact, 'One analysis of the global crop market found that pollinators are essential or highly, moderately, or slightly necessary for 91 crops consumed by humans.'"[117]

With regard to forests/jungles/rain forests, here are some statistics that show the incredibly resourceful and ingenious power of God, as well as the importance of His creation to us:

- "A single mature tree can absorb carbon dioxide at a rate of 48 lbs./year and release enough oxygen back into the atmosphere to support 2 human beings" (Arguments for Land Conservation: Documentation and Information Sources for Land Resources Protection, Trust for Public Land).

- "One acre of trees annually consumes the amount of carbon dioxide equivalent to that produced by driving an average car for 26,000 miles. That same acre of trees also produces enough oxygen for 18 people to breathe for a year" (New York Times).

- "A 100-ft tree, 18-inch diameter at its base, produces 6,000 pounds of oxygen" (Northwest Territories Forest Management).

- "On average, one tree produces nearly 260 pounds of oxygen each year. Two mature trees can provide enough oxygen for a family of four" (Canada's National Environmental Agency).[118]

Clearly, there's a lot of oxygen being produced by trees. But this amount pales in comparison to what is produced by ocean plant life. "It is estimated that marine plants produce between 70 and 80 percent of the oxygen in the atmosphere. . . . Think about it, 70 percent to 80 percent of all the oxygen we breathe comes from algae! Without them we would really be sucking wind, but not for long!"[119] Our plants (on land and sea) are vital to us.

The third environmental problem afflicting our planet is *soil degradation.* For decades it's been increasing due to "[o]vergrazing, monoculture planting, erosion, soil compaction, overexposure to pollutants, land-use conversion."[120] According to the World Wildlife Fund, "[h]alf of the topsoil on the planet has been lost in the last 150 years," which "is a primary concern to farmers and the global community whose livelihoods depend on well managed agriculture that starts with the dirt beneath our feet."[121] Obviously, if Earth's soil is not healthy, then a plentiful supply of food can't be grown in order to sustain human life.

All of these problems do not paint a very bright picture. And everything gets even darker when we consider the state of persons who must endure their personal suffering, fear, hopelessness, frustration, and helplessness without Christ. In the midst of so much turmoil and pain there is only one deliverer—Jesus. And people need to meet Him. Is there anything more worthy at this time in history than reaching out to as many as possible with the gospel of peace?

## GET INVOLVED IN WHAT GOD IS DOING

Participating in the Great Commission is the obligation of every Christian. A lot of Christians, however, approach it in a somewhat backward way. Many people want to go on a mission trips globally, before even going on missions locally (e.g., around their neighborhoods, at work, in school, sometimes even in their own families).

*Question:* If you haven't yet begun to share the gospel locally, how can you go on a mission trip to spread the gospel globally?

*Answer:* You can't.

Sharing your faith follows a pattern laid down by Jesus Himself when he issued the Great Commission. It progresses in natural steps that our Lord spelled out in Acts 1:8—from Jerusalem, to Judea and Samaria, and finally, throughout the ends of the earth.

First, Jerusalem symbolizes where we're supposed to set up the framework of what will eventually be our global ministry. It starts with us witnessing/ministering to those in our immediate community; we must begin with those who are closest to us. Jesus told His disciples that Jerusalem would be where they'd receive the Holy Spirit's power (Acts 1:8). But why Jerusalem? Because it was where they'd fallen, run away, and failed. It was their place of utter weakness. That is always a perfect place for a believer to begin working for God, whose "power works best in weakness" (2 Cor. 12:9). Our Jerusalem marks the place where each of us are to begin the journey of ministry.

Next, Judea and Samaria represent those areas just beyond our personal locality. Such places might best be thought of as follows: *primarily*, in regional/national terms (i.e., geographically); and *secondarily*, in terms of anywhere outside our comfort zone (i.e., spiritually, emotionally, and psychologically). The secondary meaning is particularly fascinating when considering Samaria. It was an area quite hostile to Jews (and vice-versa, see Luke 9:53–54). Jews considered Samaritans to be half-breeds unworthy of God's promises. As such, they were to be avoided (see John 4:9). Despite this unfriendly relationship between Jews and Samaritans (in our lives, perhaps analogous to Christians and Secularists), believers were told that reaching out to Samaria/Samaritans was the next step in spreading the gospel. We, too, have a responsibility to preach in areas that might be extremely uncomfortable (not just geographically, but personally/relationally—e.g., to a hostile neighbor, or to an estranged family member).

Finally, we have the "ends of the earth," which is most commonly interpreted as global missions. Pastor and author, John Piper, has made some very interesting remarks on this topic, basing his views on Acts 1:1–11 ("you will receive power when the Holy Spirit comes upon you. And you will be my witnesses, telling people about me everywhere. . . . to the ends of the earth") and Luke 24:47–49 ("this message would be proclaimed in the authority of his name to all the nations, beginning in Jerusalem. . . . But stay here in the city until the Holy Spirit comes and fills you with power from heaven"). According to Piper, what is most crucial regarding this aspect of the Great Commission is the *power* needed to accomplish the task at hand:

> Special power is essential for an expanding witness to Christ. The reason I say power is essential for witness is because in both Luke 24:49 and Acts 1:8 Jesus says that power must come first. . . . The reason I say this power is essential for an expanding witness to Christ is because in both these texts Jesus is sending them from Jerusalem in ever-expanding circles. . . . Jesus is not talking here of an occasional word of witness in our same circle of culture.

He's talking about ever-expanding efforts to penetrate more and more of Satan's strongholds of unbelief. . . . The reason I say special power is essential is that it takes power just to become a Christian. But it takes another dimension of power to carry out an expanding witness to Christ. . . . Jesus telling them to wait for is special power—something more than the ordinary experience of power that makes a person a Christian and makes him love/worship and have joy and go to prayer.[122]

In this message, which Piper delivered on October 16, 1988, he goes on to outline exactly what the Lord's "power" does for us (or what it produces in us).

First, "when the Holy Spirit falls upon you in power, your witness to Christ comes with deep conviction [see 1 Thess. 1:5]."[123]

Second, "when the Holy Spirit falls upon you in power your witness to Christ comes with self-denying courage and boldness [see Acts 4:31; 2 Tim. 1:7–8]. Where does boldness come from? It comes from the fullness of the Holy Spirit. Where does courage to suffer for Christ come from? It comes from the power of God—the Spirit of power!"[124]

Third, "when the Holy Spirit falls upon you in power your witness to Christ comes with convincing wisdom, irresistible words [see Acts 6:5–8]. . . . If the power of the Holy Spirit comes down and you are clothed with heavenly wisdom, something supernatural will happen. Your words will carry an irresistible force."[125]

Fourth, "when the Holy Spirit falls upon you in power your witness to Christ comes with converting effectiveness [see Luke 1:15–17; Acts 11:24]. . . . We need the special power of the Spirit's fullness because the human heart is so hard to turn to God! Conversions are the work of God."[126]

The overall thrust of Piper's message is that God is the one who enables us to succeed on every level of missions. This is often why, when we least expect God to move, that is when He decides to move the most. I remember, for instance, a few years ago, when I had gone to the Middle East on a mission trip with my friend, Pastor Fady Ghobrial. We went to Ramallah in the West Bank, and we were doing some sound testing before the main event at the hotel. Fady got up and started checking the microphone by simply reciting from chapter one of John's Gospel. Suddenly, while he was speaking, out from the kitchen came three people who had been cooking the meal for that night's Christmas celebration. And they began walking forward to the front of the room, obviously moved by the verses.

When Fady had finished testing the equipment, they asked, "Can you please repeat those words again? It was giving us great comfort and hope." (Remember, they weren't even in the room when Fady began speaking. They were back in the kitchen and only heard him from a distance. Yet the Spirit drew them near.)

Fady wasn't preaching. He wasn't trying to make a doctrinal point. He wasn't telling a story to illustrate a deep truth or a profound message. He was just reciting God's Word. But the Spirit was miraculously working in their hearts, just as scripture tells us: "[F]aith comes from hearing, that is, hearing the Good News about Christ" (Rom. 10:17).

But this isn't the end of the story.

Fady approached me, asking: "Can I borrow your Bible?"

"Sure," I said, not knowing what was about to happen.

So, I handed him my Bible, complete with years of copious notes written diligently on countless pages. At that point, Fady began quoting verse after verse, leading these three people along the Roman Road of Salvation: Romans 3:10–12; Romans 3:23; Romans 6:23; Romans 5:8; Romans 10:9–13; Romans 5:1; Romans 8:1; and Romans 8:38–39.

Finally, after Fady had finished, one of the three (a cook) asked, "Can I have that book?"

My heart stopped, frozen in disbelief and trepidation. I looked at Fady, who without even asking me, casually and joyously answered, "OF COURSE!"

Well, needless to say, that was the last I saw of my Bible. But I had no other choice. We hadn't brought any extra Bibles. Our purpose at that location was to simply hold a Christmas service. We didn't think we'd need any Bibles to give away. So, with a heavy sigh, I smiled and said goodbye to my treasured possession. I still wonder sometimes where my Bible might be—how far it's traveled and who might own it. I realize, of course, I'll never know any of those things. But I do know that God is using it somewhere and somehow to change someone's life.

## EXTEND CHRIST'S LOVE TO OTHERS

During my many international trips, I've seen countless persons lacking adequate medical care, clean water, nutritious food, basic clothing, good shelter, and just about everything else necessary for a safe and healthy life. And it's certainly important that Christians help in providing these necessities. But our responsibilities don't stop with taking care of physical needs. Our greatest, and most pressing, obligation is to offer the gospel. Let me be clear—I'm not saying that supplying physical assistance is unimportant. I'm saying that supplying physical assistance, *from an eternal/spiritual perspective,* isn't as crucial as imparting spiritual truths. Meeting one's physical needs can only give temporal comfort (which, of course, is needed), but introducing someone to the gospel can bring eternal peace.

Today we're in a "Kingdom Emergency." What I mean is that the world's population is growing at a faster rate than the pace at which we're sharing the gospel. There are currently "1,510 Unengaged, Unreached People Groups who are still beyond the reach of the gospel. . . . These approximately 46 million people are spiritually lost and helpless. . . . They are unengaged, which means that no church, no mission agency—no one has yet taken responsibility to tell them of our great God and Saviour. . . . These 1,510 are at the very heart of the unfinished Great Commission task."[127] They have "no known full-time workers involved in evangelism and church planting."[128] All of these groups suffer under a stunning lack of resources.[129]

Paul Eshleman—Director of Finishing the Task Ministry—has observed, "As you look at the current list of unengaged people groups, it is shattering to realize that after 2,000 years there is still no one seeking to reach them."[130] Equally striking is the calculation of how many more workers must be mobilized in order to effectively reach the current number of unengaged, unreached people groups: 10,000. This is based on the estimation that a minimum of one full-time worker is needed for every 50,000 people in order to engage them adequately.[131]

It's unbelievable to me that so many people remain unmoved by this global need. To not feel anything for these lost groups shows, in my opinion, a lack of true appreciation for Christ's death for the world (John 3:16). I don't mean to sound harsh. But my bluntness arises out of the deep anguish I feel over the sheer number of persons who, at least at this point in time, have no chance of hearing about Jesus and His loving sacrifice for them (Rom. 5:8). It's especially troubling when one looks at the number of Christians available across the globe.

As of 2017, there were millions of Christian churches worldwide that contributed to the existence of approximately 41,000 Christian denominations, which are split into some 300 major ecclesiastical traditions scattered throughout 238 countries.[132] Furthermore, "Christianity is ranked the largest religion in the world today. According to the Pew Forum on Religion and Public Life, in 2010 there were 2.18 billion Christians around the world, nearly a third of the global population."[133] Consider, too, the following statistics:

- There are 20,500 full-time Christian workers and 10,200 foreign missionaries working throughout the unevangelized world.

- There are 1.31 million full-time Christian workers in the evangelized non-Christian world.

- There are 306,000 foreign missionaries to other Christian lands in the Christian world.[134]

And yet, despite these numbers, at last count approximately 2 billion (1 in 4 individuals) had not yet heard the gospel![135] And if you add to this figure, the number of people who have heard the gospel, but who have not yet accepted Christ as their Savior, you get a total of 3.5 to 4 billion people who are not Christian! This is tragic. Clearly, the Great Commission is not being fulfilled. According to the Issachar Initiative, the current situation might be due to the fact that "99.7% of missional activities and financial support are directed toward where the church ALREADY IS. Only 0.3% of resources are allocated to where the church is NOT."[136]

When I look at these numbers, my heart burns with an overwhelming desire to do something about it. I simply can't put myself into a little bubble wherein I'm only concerned about *my* church, *my* community, *my* family—not while the rest of the world is dying without Christ. The state of the world should burden all of our hearts so heavily that we're compelled to do something. We must all see the world as God sees it. It's a world filled with the hopeless and the helpless, who are in desperate need of Christ as their Savior.

## ACT NOW; ACT QUICKLY

But all is not lost. There is an upside. We live in an era of unprecedented technology and opportunities for the spreading the gospel. For example, each of us now enjoys a life expectancy far beyond the life expectancy of people just one hundred years ago (70–80 years old vs. 25–40 years old). That gives us more time to do God's work. We also have mass communication. Other advantages today include better health, more political freedom, better education, and a much greater understanding of the world in general. We have *everything* we need to get the job done; most significantly, we have God's Word, power, love, strength, and blessings.

So, what excuse is there for not spreading the gospel? There isn't one; except perhaps if a Christian, for some reason, doesn't think the Great Commission is a priority. Jesus' last words, of course, make it a priority: "'[Y]ou will be my witnesses, telling people about me everywhere—in Jerusalem, throughout Judea, in Samaria, and to the ends of the earth'" (Acts 1:8). If we're true followers of Christ, and we want to be seen as His true followers, then we must contribute in some way to spreading the gospel on a global scale. There's no other option.

Jesus is the answer—regardless of how events may transpire for those languishing in the world, no matter how difficult their circumstances may be, whatever horrible experiences they might be forced to endure. Yes, Jesus is the answer. No matter what someone might be physically suffering, there always has been (and always will be) spiritual peace, joy, hope, comfort, strength, and purpose to be found in Christ. This is evident in countless stories of healing received by those who have accepted Jesus as their savior. "'Come to me, all of you who are weary and carry heavy burdens, and I will give you rest'" (Matt. 11:28).

I like to say: "You can't enjoy Kingdom privileges without also embracing Kingdom obligations."

In other words, Kingdom privileges go hand-in-hand with Kingdom obligations, just like the Old Testament goes hand-in-hand with the New Testament. Moreover, from a purely ethical/moral standpoint, it's not right to expect others to do all the work. And there's a lot of work to still do. You, as a NextGen leader, can be part of a team that helps fulfill the Great Commission. You can complete the circle of ministry that right now remains unclosed. You can change the course of world history. And you can do it by developing a personal ministry plan.

---- **8** ----

# DEVELOP A PERSONAL PLAN

A pilot without a plane is called a pedestrian.
A coach without a team is called a fan.
A business without a delivery system is called a warehouse.
A gathering of Christians without a way to link with other ministries
is called a local church. We cannot fulfill our potential
without an appropriate vehicle of transport beyond ourselves. . . .
Most local churches have become so preoccupied with catering
to the needs of those who meet in the church building
that they have forgotten the potential of love.

— Joel C. Hunter —
Northland, A Church Distributed[137]

I n July 2016, I met a young man named Ali, an Iraqi refugee who had been received into the home a Christian family in Dallas, TX. When only 18-years-old, this young man lost both of his parents in Baghdad, Iraq, during the suicide bombing of a street market. Within a few seconds he suddenly became an orphan with no home, no siblings, and no other relatives.

His journey to America was long and arduous, beginning in Turkey, where he arrived not long after his mother and father were killed. His vetting process there lasted for nearly four years. But finally, after being thoroughly investigated, he was cleared to enter the United States.

I met him the night I spoke at a church located near the family hosting him. They decided to bring him to hear me speak because they found out I'd be sharing my message at an Arabic meeting. His hosts thought it would be a good idea to help Ali find others with whom he could identify. So, they all jumped into the car and showed up to hear me speak.

At church, I was the first person to greet him. I, of course, welcomed him warmly and began introducing him to others. The first thing about him that I immediately noticed was his fear. He was very scared, spoke almost no English, and didn't know what to say to me. He seemed afraid of everyone as he stood there uncomfortably, his eyes darting back and forth. I couldn't blame him. He had often experienced death threats because his father was Shi'ite Muslim and his mother was a Sunni Muslim—i.e., two branches of Islam in great conflict.

Eventually, the service started. And I decided on the spot to begin my message by introducing my new friend. "Dear brothers and sisters, tonight we have a special guest with us," I said. "He's come to us from Iraq and his name is Ali."

His name, of course, is very Muslim-sounding, so everyone perked up and paid attention.

I continued. "Ali is an orphan. He lost his mom and dad in a car bombing in the market of Baghdad. He has no aunts or uncles, and no cousins."

Then, I looked at Ali, and said, "You lost your family. And you're an only child. You lost everything. But I want to tell you right here, from this pulpit, from this moment on, this church is now your family. And you have new brothers and new sisters." I then spoke in Arabic, looking straight at Ali, saying, "Ali, I don't ever want you to forget this verse." And I read the passage God had given me while I was praying before the service: "For I assisted the poor in their need, and the orphans who required help" (Job 29:12). Turning my attention back to Ali, I said, "Ali, we love you. We are here for you."

As soon as I said those words, this lonely young man began weeping like a baby. He knew he was safe. He knew he was loved. He knew he was accepted by us, and accepted by God.

Later, Ali sent me a message, saying, "Fares, I had always heard about Jesus' love. But today I saw it. I touched it. It became real to me."

In this story we see the fertile ground for evangelism in the lives of those who have been emotionally wounded, spiritually broken, and psychologically traumatized by the horrors of the Middle East. Men, women, and children in the Levant need Jesus. But unless we're willing to move beyond our comfort zone and reach out to them with our time, talent, and treasure, they will have no hope of deliverance in Christ. And we will never be able to fulfill our Lord's Great Commission to save all nations through the good news. But how does a faithful follower of Jesus actually develop a ministry designed to help the lost? This will be the focus of our final chapter, which I hope will assist you, step-by-step, in creating your own worldwide ministry.

## SUPPORT A MINISTRY

One of the best ways to move toward having your own ministry is by first supporting a ministry that already exists. Irreplaceable are the steadfast brothers and sisters who pray for a ministry, contribute financially to a ministry, or provide another kind of help (e.g., donating missionary supplies, volunteering time, hosting guest speakers). Without such support, running a ministry would be impossible. John Chrysostom (c. 349–407), Archbishop of Constantinople, noted the hardships of ministry in the fourth century: "I know my own soul, how feeble and puny it is: I know the magnitude of this ministry, and the great difficulty of the work; for more stormy billows vex the soul of the priest than the gales which disturb the sea."

## GIVE GENEROUSLY

Financial support is perhaps the most popular way of helping a ministry. We see it in several biblical passages, including Luke 8:1–3, where Jesus' ministry is given financial assistance. However, the most well-known verse dealing with financial gifts comes from Paul: "What soldier has to pay his own expenses? What farmer plants a vineyard and doesn't have the right to eat some of its fruit? What shepherd cares for a flock of sheep and isn't allowed to drink some of the milk? Am I expressing merely a human opinion, or does the law say the same thing? For the law of Moses says, 'You must not muzzle an ox to keep it from eating as it treads out the grain.' Was God thinking only about oxen when he said this? Wasn't he actually speaking to us? Yes, it was written for us, so that the one who plows and the one who threshes the grain might both expect a share of the harvest" (1 Cor. 9:7–11; see also 1 Tim. 5:17–18).

The key phrase here is "You must not muzzle an ox to keep it from eating as it treads out the grain," which is from Deuteronomy 25:4. It's a reference to how oxen were used to separate the grain from the chaff by walking on the grains. The animals were allowed to simply take a mouthful of the grain whenever they felt inclined to do so. This imagery serves to point out how ministers of the gospel should be given whatever they need to survive and perform their duties. It's a fitting allegory to how persons in ministry should receive financial support for their efforts.

Of course, not everyone can give financially to a ministry. Some of Jesus' supporters, for example, instead of providing direct funds, offered their homes as a place for the disciples to stay during missionary excursions (Luke 10:5–10; see also Matt. 10:5–14). This form of support was given quite often during biblical times (see Acts 9:43, 10:47–48, 16:15, 17:4–5, 18:1–3, 7, 21:15–16). It's still rather common today. In fact, there actually exists an international directory of homes that are open for "providing rest and renewal for full-time pastors, clergy, missionaries, chaplains, ministry directors, and other full-time Christian workers."[138]

Other types of generous giving would be contributions of stocks, bonds, life insurance, valuable possessions (e.g., an automobile, real estate, computers, cameras), and even particulars of an estate that are listed in a will. Sometimes such donations can have significant tax benefits. For example, "[a] residence, vacation home, farm, acreage, or vacant lot may have so appreciated in value through the years that its sale would mean a sizeable capital gains tax. By making a gift of this property instead, you would avoid the capital gains tax, and, at the same time, receive a charitable deduction for the full fair market value of the property."[139]

## PRAY INTENTIONALLY

Both financial support and hospitality support are certainly needed, but I believe that prayer support is even more crucial. I've been so blessed when, at the end of a message I've delivered as a guest speaker, someone has come up to me, saying, "Fares, we've been praying for you ever since the last time you were here." I can't put into words the comfort and joy I've felt when these cherished prayer warriors have told me how faithfully they've continued to lift up my needs to God. In some cases, I had expressed my needs to that church several *years* earlier.

This type of support can really give fuel to a leader's engine because it not only gives moral support, but it actually releases God's power. It's a sobering and humbling thought to know there are people out there dedicated to praying for you! Our Lord can certainly do all things, even without our prayers, because He's sovereign (Jer. 32:27; Job 42:2; Dan. 4:35; Matt. 19:26). But what's beautiful and awe-inspiring is how God *chooses* to work *through* our prayers. In this way, He allows us to participate in His plans for the world.

Such support reminds me of Aaron and Hur, who helped Moses during the war between the Israelites (led by Joshua) and the Amalekites (led by Amalek). As Joshua went forward, Moses, Aaron, and Hur went to the top of a hill to watch the battle. When Moses held his hands up, Israel prevailed. But when Moses let his hand down, Amalek prevailed (Ex. 17:11). Eventually, Moses couldn't hold up his hands any longer. That's when Aaron and Hur helped: "Aaron and Hur found a stone for him to sit on. Then they stood on each side of Moses, holding up his hands. So his hands held steady until sunset." (v. 12).

Kevin DeYoung—Reformed Evangelical theologian/author and senior pastor of Christ Covenant Church—made some interesting observations about this kind of prayer support in a July 12, 2016 message on Moses, Aaron, and Hur:

> In Luke 22:32, Jesus told Peter, "Go and strengthen the brothers." In Acts 18:23, Paul traveled back and strengthened all the disciples. . . . We need each other. We need people to say, "I'll pray for you when you run out of prayers. I'll keep praying for that when your prayers have turned into anxiety." . . . God is calling some of you this week to be Aaron and Hur. God wants others to admit that they are Moses in this moment. Sometimes it's harder to admit that you are Moses—not the one who sends the plagues and leads the people. We love that Moses. But what about this Moses? Can you admit, "I can't keep my hands up by myself anymore. I can't do it?"

Right now you might be someone who's either: a) in ministry and desperately in need of prayer support; or b) not currently in ministry, but you want to help.

For those in the first group, I urge you to make your needs known. Reach out to your church. Call friends and family. Humble yourself and be honest about the support you need because of fatigue, worry, doubts, or perhaps just boredom. Don't be afraid to be vulnerable and express your heart to those around you. Trust me, there are many people who will joyfully be an Aaron or a Hur to you. One truly amazing aspect of being in "fellowship" with each other (Acts 2:42) is our access to others who will help us in our times of weakness.

For those in the second group, you're needed. The time has come for you, at the very least, to make a commitment to those in ministry. You can make a significant difference in what's happening at your church, in your community, and throughout your country. Your prayers can even make a difference around the entire globe. Hopefully, when the time is right, the day will come when you, too, will feel moved to actually join a ministry.

## JOIN A MINISTRY

Joining a ministry is step two in the process of ministerial involvement. It's when you become even more connected to the work of the Church through hands-on participation. Joining a ministry allows you to share more of your time, treasure, and talent with the world. Think of it as becoming part of a sports team after being a fan. It takes you out of the cheering stands and puts you onto the playing field. You actually become one of the players! It certainly means greater work, commitment, sacrifice, and discipline—but it also means greater rewards.

Your activities as a team member will be far more varied than those of a supporter. As a supporter, you only make generalized contributions such as prayer, finances, or tangible supplies. As a team member, however, you make very personal contributions that are unique to your own gifts (e.g., talent to lead worship, administrative/organizational acumen, public speaking skills). You might also have to go to meetings on a regular basis, or there might be mission trips to go on, and there could be events to attend such as local conferences or community outreaches.

Several scriptures apply to joining a ministry. First, "'Come, all of you who are gifted craftsmen. Construct everything that the Lord has commanded'" (Ex. 35:10). Second, "Give as freely as you have received!" (Matt. 10:8). Third, "There are different kinds of service, but we serve the same Lord. God works in different ways, but it is the same God who does the work in all of us." (1 Cor. 12:5–6). Fourth, "God has given each of you a gift from his great variety of spiritual gifts. Use them well to serve one another. Do you have the gift of speaking? Then speak as though God himself were speaking through you. Do you have the gift of helping others? Do it with all the strength and energy that God supplies. Then everything you do will bring glory to God through Jesus Christ. All glory and power to him forever and ever!" (1 Peter 4:10–11).

### SERVE PASSIONATELY

Right about now you might be asking yourself what many people ask themselves: *How do I know which ministry to join?* Basically, you have to figure out the specific issue you feel most passionate about. Everyone's passionate about something. And as a Christian, you're going to be passionate about some aspect of God's work. Your passion is the Holy Spirit moving in you, drawing you into service. Just remember that your passion must be *your* passion, not someone else's passion. We each have our own calling/passion. That's a truth easily forgotten.

I recall how one time I attended a missions conference, where I met several financial donors. It was great to see so many people dedicated to helping ministries achieve the dreams that God had imparted to various ministry leaders. I was so excited, particularly when I was given the opportunity to spend nearly forty-five minutes sharing my heart—i.e., my burden for the Levant, my concern for the Middle East, and my commitment to use Levant Ministries to spread the gospel, especially through future outreaches. Many people wanted to help. And I was blessed. But there was also one man, who surprised me, and not in a good way. He came up to me and said, "You know, Fares, I appreciate all you said. I love what you're doing. But to be honest, my heart is in India."

To tell the truth, I was a little upset. I thought, *Wow, after all I said, the guy still isn't interested; he's not interested at all in making an investment in the kingdom.* But after going back to my hotel room, and thinking about it (then praying about it), I realized: *Hey, wait a minute. All this guy was saying is that his heart is not in the Middle East. His passion burns for India. God bless him.* I suddenly became overjoyed about his calling. He wasn't doing what I was doing, but he was still working for the Kingdom. He was joining somewhere. And even though I was working in a totally different area of world ministry, he still took the time to listen to me. This showed me that although he was focused on his own passion, he was still keeping his heart open.

All of us, just like this dear brother, must find and focus on our passion, while still remaining flexible to God's leading. Here we see the truth of Paul's words about the Church in First Corinthians 12:15–26:

> If the foot says, "I am not a part of the body because I am not a hand," that does not make it any less a part of the body. And if the ear says, "I am not part of the body because I am not an eye," would that make it any less a part of the body? If the whole body were an eye, how would you hear? Or if your whole body were an ear, how would you smell anything? But our bodies have many parts, and God has put each part just where he wants it. How strange a body would be if it had only one part! Yes, there are many parts, but only one body. The eye can never say to the hand, "I don't need you." The head can't say to the feet, "I don't need you." . . . God has put the body together such that extra honor and care are given to those parts that have less dignity. This makes for harmony among the members, so that all the members care for each other. If one part suffers, all the parts suffer with it, and if one part is honored, all the parts are glad.

There are so many different ministries, causes, programs, organizations, and groups working for God. Some reach out to women. Others train young people and/or children. Many focus on specific countries/continents such as China, Russia, Africa, or South America. All of them are filled with brothers and sisters who have a passion to serve in that particular area.

Every Christian will be pulled by God toward a passion. And He usually bases that pull on our experiences, personality, talents/gifts, and knowledge received through education. This pull then presents us with a choice. We can either: a) shut it down and do nothing; or b) pursue it, allowing the Spirit to convict our hearts, and say, "Ok, God's speaking to me (through another believer, a project, or ministry) and I must connect to it, join up to be part of what God's doing."

## FOLLOW GOD'S LEAD

This doesn't mean you need to look for a perfect ministry. Just like searching for a church (see Chapter One), the point is not to find a place that's *perfect*, but rather, to find a place (or ministry) that's *perfect for you*. Sometimes God might call you to join (or perhaps support) a ministry that's well-established. Or, He might call you to join a ministry still crawling along its way, perhaps even one that's just starting out and struggling. The latter kind of ministry can often lead to some of the most rewarding experiences you'll ever have in life. You might actually be the one God is calling to help such a ministry become something truly spectacular!

Basically, you have to be sensitive to the Spirit. You have to be intentional about what you do. You have to have your priorities in the proper order. And your number one priority can't be success at school, getting ahead in your career, or even finding a spouse. All of those things, of course, are important and deserve attention. But if you're a Christian, then your first priority, far above anything else, needs to be following Jesus Christ and serving Him with all your heart, soul, mind, and strength (Mark 12:30–31). The Lord must be your first love (Rev. 2:4–5).

God can accomplish unbelievable things with people totally committed to His work. Levant Ministries has been blessed with a wide variety of persons who have contributed wonderful gifts that have helped its success. Consider my friend, Tony Nijmeh. He's not only a board member, but is one of my closest advisors. In fact, before making any decisions, I consult Tony. I ask for his wisdom and insights; he always delivers. Sometimes, to be honest, what he says to me isn't necessarily what I want to hear. But without fail, it's the answer that

I need to be given, even when it goes against my personal ambitions and/or feelings.

This can sometimes be uncomfortable, but it's a good thing. Leaders need contrary voices to offset places where they might be blind or weak. There is nothing quite as helpful as a member of the ministry who tells it like it is because: 1) they care about the ministry succeeding; 2) they believe honesty is the best way to help; and 3) they share the same values/principles as the ministry leader. Remember, as a ministry participant (and leader), your overriding concern must be how can the ministry succeed *for* God—using God's resources, in God's way, according to God's timetable. It's not about you, or what you necessarily want. It's about what God wants. And a trusted advisor on the team is one sure way to make this happen. As scripture tells us, "Plans go wrong for lack of advice; many advisers bring success" (Prov. 15:22).

So, if you're the kind of person who has great insight and wisdom, then that is a perfect reason for you to join a ministry. Whatever your gifts might be, all it takes is one step to join a ministry. Don't be afraid to answer God, just as Samuel answered the Lord when He called to him, "Samuel! Samuel!" Then, Samuel said, "Speak, your servant is listening" (1 Sam. 3:10).

## START A MINISTRY

Eventually, after experiencing what it's like to join a ministry, you'll at some point likely feel comfortable enough to start your own ministry/outreach. In my opinion, this is where the real fun begins. But it's also where the real work begins.

I won't lie. It can be tough to start a new ministry. Sometimes, in fact, I look back to the beginnings of Levant Ministries and I'm not quite sure how I did it. Or, perhaps more accurately, I'm not sure how I succeeded in doing it. But this, in reality, is a probably good sign. It tells me that God made it all happen. He alone, therefore, gets all the glory, honor, and praise—all of it. Levant Ministries exists not only *for* Him, but completely and totally 100% *because* of Him.

There were certain steps, of course, that I obviously needed to take to get the ministry up and running. My hope is to share with you these steps so that you, too, can begin a ministry.

## STEP ONE: WATCH AND LEARN

First, I just watched people—specifically, ministry leaders. I observed how they ran their ministries, taking special note of the difficulties they encountered. I also studied what they did to overcome these difficulties, paying close attention to how they: 1) reacted to setbacks; 2) altered their plans; 3) inspired others; 4) pursued their dream; 5) managed their time; 6) made decisions; and 7) trusted God. "Let the wise listen to these proverbs and become even wiser. Let those with understanding receive guidance," says Proverbs 1:5. Similarly, Proverbs 18:15 reads, "Intelligent people are always ready to learn. Their ears are open for knowledge."

Everything I saw increased my understanding of life in ministry. Even the mistakes I watched being made by leaders taught me a lot. In fact, their missteps taught me more than their successes. Initially, I viewed the errors rather incredulously (and naively), asking myself: *How could anyone make such an obvious mistake?* But then, after growing in my knowledge of the ministerial world, my heart changed. I learned that the errors I saw leaders making were actually quite easy to make. That's when I began asking myself: *How can I avoid doing that?* This put me on my guard, which has helped me avoid all kinds of problems: problems in my way because of the Enemy, as well as those set in my path by my own frailties and sinfulness (Jer. 17:9).

Pastor Chris Hodges (Church of the Highlands) has come up with an ingenious way to make sure all of his leaders have taken this step, which he himself still practices. "I constantly learn from churches that do things better than us," he explains. "In fact, I require every person on my team who leads a ministry or department to connect with three people in the nation who do their jobs as well or better than them."[140]

## STEP TWO: PRAY WITHOUT CEASING

Second, I prayed constantly (see Chapter Four). As I've discussed elsewhere in this volume, the importance of having a solid prayer life cannot be overstated, especially when you're in ministry. In *The Power of Prayer and the Prayer of Power,* the famous Christian author, pastor, and evangelist, R.A. Torrey, had this to say about prayer:

> Prayer is the key that unlocks all the storehouses of God's infinite grace and power. All that God is, and all that God has, is at the disposal of prayer. But we must use the key. . . . No one can stand against the man [or woman, or child] who knows how to pray and who meets all the conditions of prevailing prayer and who really prays.[141]

I've repeatedly seen for myself the truthfulness of Torrey's assertion. This is why, when I prayed about starting Levant Ministries I prayed not only about the obvious issues (guidance, strength, inspiration, assistance, patience, direction, finances, and divine favor), but I also prayed about the less obvious issues. I prayed that I wouldn't just copy whomever I had been watching. This might seem like the opposite of what I recommended in the previous step, but it's not. It's complementary. You want to *learn* from others, but you don't want to become others. God has uniquely created you with specific talents, characteristics, strengths, experiences, passions, and insights. And He wants to use your unique qualities for a unique purpose.

Even the writers of God's Word, as the Holy Spirit spoke through them (2 Peter 1:21), communicated the mind of God using their own background, knowledge, experiences, temperament, linguistic skills, vocabulary, and personality. Paul didn't write like Peter. John didn't write like Matthew. Luke didn't write like James. Yet all of them helped author God's Word to humanity. They each had their role to play based on their unique identity. You, too, have your own contribution to make to God's ministerial community based on your unique identity.

God wired you a certain way; He designed you a certain way; He implanted within you certain attributes that are usable only through you. In other words, STEP ONE is about seeing the greatness in others, while STEP TWO is about discovering the greatness in you. This not only glorifies God, but accomplishes His will in His way. "You made all the delicate, inner parts of my body and knit me together in my mother's womb. Thank you for making me so wonderfully complex! Your workmanship is marvelous—how well I know it" (Psalm 139:13–14). Only you can do what God wants you to do in the world. *So, be yourself!*

## STEP THREE: DO YOUR HOMEWORK

Third, I did research. You must take a good look at the area of ministry to which you're feeling called: women, missions/evangelism, children, special needs groups, substance abuse, veterans, music/worship, counseling, dating/marriage. There are an unlimited number of ministries available to you in today's church. But wherever you feel God is leading you, you must survey that territory. Think back on how the Israelites conquered the land that God had placed before them. They didn't just say, "Let's go," then run wildly and haphazardly into battle. Joshua took the time to send spies into the land to see *exactly* what the Lord's people would be facing (Jos 2:1). This didn't mean he lacked faith in God's promises. On the contrary, it showed that he possessed great faith. It also showed that he had great wisdom and insight:

> While Joshua had the promise of God's deliverance, he had not been given instruction on just how God would defeat the enemies they would face. As a wise military leader, he was simply gathering information concerning the layout of the [enemy's] defenses, the condition of their [morale], and other factors that would be important to any military campaign. Moreover he was not to presume on the Lord. He was to trust the Lord implicitly, but in that trust, he was also to use the resources God gave him: the training, the men, and the wisdom he had gained. See Matt. 4:6-7. . . . Faith looks for the principles of Scripture that might be applicable, gathers information or the facts needed in making wise decisions, and then, based on biblical principles and the facts known, moves ahead trusting in the provision and directions of the Lord (cf. Luke 14:31).[142]

Next, after you've done research, before you ask anyone to donate anything, ask yourself: *Why should they give their hard-earned money to me?* Before asking volunteers to volunteer, ask yourself: *Why should they give their time, talent, and treasure to my fledgling ministry, instead of giving their time, talent, and treasure to another ministry that is already established and successful?* Before asking others to share your vision, ask yourself: *Why should they believe that I can, as Joshua did, successfully take the land God has promised? Has God even made any promises to me about this area of ministry, or any promises about this land I plan to conquer?*

You have to work your way through a lot of tough questions that you might naturally want to avoid. But there can be no shortcuts taken in this area. Surveying the territory of your ministry, and your approach to conquering it, is the mark of a good leader who's ready to lead. Looking over the various aspects of a creating new ministry in a particular field will also help you be a good steward of whatever resources come your way. No one takes a road trip without first consulting a map, choosing a route, allowing for rest stops, planning for meals, and reserving places to stay. And starting a new ministry is a lot more complex than taking a road trip!

## STEP FOUR: DEFINE YOUR VISION AND MISSION

Fourth, I outlined my long-term and short-term goals. Before making any fundraising attempts or seeking any volunteers, I realized I needed to write my God-inspired dream on paper. I had to put it into a concrete form. I split this process into two parts: 1) a "Vision Statement"; and 2) a "Mission Statement." These are two of the most important preparations to make during the creation of a new ministry.

A **Vision Statement** establishes your end-goal. What are you hoping to accomplish? What is your final destination? What legacy do you want to leave behind? By answering these questions, you'll be able to both see and communicate in clear detail when "success" has been reached. Writing a Vision Statement can be a difficult. In fact, ministries aren't alone in this struggle. Businesses also have a difficult time of it. According to *Forbes*, "[m]ost people either don't know their organization's vision, don't understand it, or feel so disconnected from it that they can't explain how it relates to their day job."[143] This article goes on to explain, "What's the 'golden rule' when crafting the vision statement? It should require effort to create, but should not require effort to understand—externally (customers) and especially internally (employees)."[144] Let's make a slight re-write: "It should require effort to create, but should not require effort to understand—externally (donors/supporters) and especially internally (volunteers/staffers)."

When it comes to ministry, if you can't articulate a precise end-goal, then you've either: a) not pushed your dream far enough (it's too small and lacks a solid conclusion); or b) pushed your dream too far (it's too big to define in concrete terms). A Vision Statement that's too small, for example, might be summarized in a way that's extremely undefined: "We want to spread the Gospel." This is an admirable desire, but it lacks specifics: Where? To whom? In what way? On the other hand, a Vision Statement that's too big might read as follows: "We want to save all unbelievers." This is a wonderful sentiment, but it's not practical. It's actually more of an open-ended hope than a true goal that can be reached by any single ministry.

I can't stress enough the importance of having a crystal-clear vision. You must focus on discerning what the *exact* goal is that God has given you to reach. All Christians are working collaboratively together to accomplish the biggest goals—e.g., fulfilling the Great Commission, establishing worldwide churches, defending the gospel, and spreading Christ's love. But what's *your* specific role within *your* personal domain when it comes to all of that activity. At Levant

Ministries, for instance, we want all Arabic-speaking people to encounter Christ. That's our vision. It's the goal we're pressing to reach. Is that the vision meant for all Christians? Of course not. It's our part of God's overall vision for humanity. Your responsibility is to find *your* part.

In "How To Write A Good Vision Statement," Tom Wright of CASCADE (an executive strategy performance company) lists six components of a good vision statement. It should be:

1) **short;**
2) **specific** to your business/ministry;
3) **devoid of unclear language** that is open to interpretation (e.g., "spread the gospel with enthusiasm," which sounds great, but doesn't really explain what is actually meant);
4) **simple** (i.e., "No technical jargon, no metaphors and no business buzz-words if at all possible");
5) **ambitious** so that it inspires/excites, but not too ambitious (e.g., anything "outside of 3 to 10 years"); and
6) **aligned** with the values you want to promote.[145]

To this advice, Shaun Spearman of Kotter International (another business guidance organization) adds another piece of wise counsel: "Visions are intended to clarify the pathway forward. When effective, the vision statement has an illuminating quality that allows organizations to move fast and with great precision. Simply stated: It's NOT complicated."[146]

As for your **Mission Statement**, this will be similar to your Vision Statement, but slightly different. Vision Statements speak in far-reaching/end-goal terms, while Mission Statements are "more concrete, and they are definitely more 'action-oriented' than vision statements. Your vision statement should inspire people to dream; your mission statement should inspire them to action."[147] This advice comes from the online Community Tool Box (CTB), a "resource for those working to build healthier communities and bring about social change."[148] According to CTB, "Having a clear mission statement can: Convert the broad dreams of your vision into more specific, action-oriented terms; Explain your goals to interested parties in a clear and concise manner; Enhance your organization's image as being competent and professional, thus reassuring funding sources that their investment was (or would be!) a smart choice."[149]

To help form any good Mission Statement, there are at least four questions that should be answered within the statement: 1) What is our goal?; 2) For whom do we do it?; 3) How do we do it?; and 4) Why do we do it? I've found that most people will have a very good understanding of a ministry if these common questions are answered clearly, concisely, and carefully. Let's consider, as a great example, the Mission Statement from my home church (Church of the Redeemer), pastored by Dale O'Shields, who puts it this way:

> The mission of Church of the Redeemer [WHAT IS OUR GOAL?] is to communicate this wonderful news of Jesus Christ [FOR WHOM DO WE DO IT?] to those who live in Montgomery County and around the world. [HOW DO WE DO IT?] We believe in the power of God's Word to change lives. We value the practical application of His Word, [WHY WE DO IT?] to make a difference in who we are and what we do. Simply put, we want to help people "connect, grow and sow"—CONNECT with God and His church, GROW into fruitful, faithful followers of Jesus, and SOW back into His Kingdom, as stated on the church website church-redeemer.org.

Interestingly, a mission statement isn't just important for those outside the ministry. It's also important, perhaps even more important, for those inside the ministry.

According to Bob Thune, lead pastor and founder of Coram Deo Church Community, "[C]lear thinking about mission is crucial to good leadership: it helps you clarify what things YOU need to do, and what things you need to empower OTHERS to do. To say it another way: God's kingdom purposes in the world—or in your city—are broader than any single church or organization. If you try to do it all, you'll end up doing nothing well. But if you stay focused on your mission—and help empower other agencies, leaders, and causes to fulfill their mission—then it really is feasible to see large-scale renewal in a city or population."[150]

This is precisely why every Mission Statement must include some kind of outline of your daily activities (e.g., projects, short-term goals, programs). These are the vehicles that will drive your ministry toward the ultimate goal presented in your Vision Statement. By outlining these activities—all of which will need budgeting, marketing, staffing, and planning—you'll help those outside *and* inside your ministry catch the vision/goal you're trying to reach.

Ministry Ventures has provided one of the best ways to delineate a Vision Statement from a Mission Statement: "**Vision**: The preferred future your organization wishes to bring about. Your vision is what you would say after you told someone to "close their eyes and imagine…"; **Mission**: The strategic focus your organization will employ in order to bring about its preferred future. Your mission is what you do."[151]

## STEP FIVE: SPREAD THE WORD AROUND

Fifth, I shared my vision/mission. Once I reached the point of needing to share my vision/mission with others, I started talking about it and never stopped. I told anyone and everyone about my dream, passion, and vision for the Levant region. To this day I still can't stop talking about it! I wake up talking about it. I go to sleep talking about it. I eat breakfast, lunch, and dinner talking about it. I keep telling my friends about it. I keep telling my pastor about it. I keep telling my neighbors about it. I keep telling strangers about it. I even keep telling my wife about it. And it drives her nuts! But I can't help myself because I'm so excited every day about what God is doing through Levant Ministries. As Craig Groeschel—senior pastor of Life.Church—wrote in his book, *It: How Churches and Leaders Can Get It and Keep It*: "Receive his vision. Let it overwhelm you. Consume you. Burden you. Tell the vision. Cast the vision. Communicate the vision. And watch *it* spread."[152]

Don't confuse what I'm saying with the cultish, doctrinally aberrant, and biblically unsound idea that a verbal confession metaphysically/magically brings possession of whatever is confessed. No. That's a belief straight out of the New Age Mind Sciences. What I'm saying is that sharing your dream/ vision: 1) "gets you started. Once you've announced it, you're accountable to try and get moving"; 2) "attracts other people's support. . . . A dream from God will attract people that you don't even know yet to help you"; and 3) "releases God's power. Because of your faith, you step out of the boat and start walking on water. God will hold you up!"[153]

We must share, share, share, then share some more. . . with everyone. We never know who's listening. It's not our job to identify the "right people" with whom we share our visions. It's our job just to share it with as many as possible. Sometimes we might even feel like we're talking to the wrong person, but in reality, we're talking to someone God has placed in front of us. This, in fact, is how I met Tony, who would eventually become one of my closest counselors/advisors.

I met Tony during a conference at which I was trying very hard to make some important connections with all of the "big guys" (e.g., large ministries, major donors, important/influential ministry leaders). I spent a lot of time and energy running around trying to meet everyone, except Tony. When it came to him, I didn't really pay attention to making a connection. I'd never heard of him before, nor did I think he was in any way associated with a ministry that might possibly be interested in the Levant region. I thought perhaps he was there representing his own fledgling ministry and, like me, was trying to raise funds from all the "big guys."

But toward the end of the conference, I finally began talking with Tony, and shared with him my hopes and dreams for Levant Ministries. He didn't say much. But we exchanged our contact information and later we re-connected over the phone. Eventually, I found out that Tony was actually praying for the right ministry to join and support. And, to make a long story short, he not only became a huge supporter for Levant Ministries, but also ended up on the ministry's Board of Directors! You never know whom you're talking to. You can't be selective, thinking to yourself, "Oh, I'm not going to share with this person; I'm not going to talk to that person."

I also learned that sharing information about God's work isn't always about getting donations or raising funds. It can simply be about spreading news that relates to His work across the globe. Moreover, as a secondary benefit, when you share your vision with others, you'll invariably get lots of feedback. This will help you refine your vision in ways that you would have likely missed on your own. Input from others is crucial.

Constantly sharing your vision/mission will also help you find volunteers you'll need to get everything up and running. Your zeal can go a long way. I learned this truth from my friend, Ronia Dubbaneh, one of our volunteers who helped me during the early stages of Levant Ministries. One day, Ronia came to me and said, "Fares, I have no idea how this thing is going to work [i.e., our first NEXTGEN Conference]. No idea at all. But I feel God's energy. I feel like God is doing something. And your passion is igniting my passion." Without even realizing it, Ronia had voiced an extraordinary truth: *Our commitment to God, to His purpose, and to His ministry will always inspire others to commit, to become passionate, to become dedicated. People can't help but be drawn to something they can sense as being greater than themselves, something that is being energized by God's Holy Spirit, something worth joining.*

## STEP SIX: RAISE RESOURCES

Sixth, I began to raise funds to make my dream/vision a reality. This was one of the most difficult and uncomfortable things I was forced to do. I don't really like talking about money, but it's a reality that every ministry leader must face. The need for financial stability is a fact of life. And if it's any comfort to you, just remember that even Moses was told by the Lord in Exodus 25:1-3 to raise funds for the tabernacle. Then, in Exodus 35, he finally asked the people to give, which they did when their "hearts were stirred" and "spirits were moved" (v. 21). And in the New Testament, Paul praised the funds raised for the Jerusalem Church (see 2 Cor. 8:6–7, 19).

In other words, fundraising shouldn't be an anxiety-ridden burden. It should be an enjoyable privilege; it's just another part of the ministry. This is where leaders get confused. Fundraising isn't a separate project to dread. It's simply another aspect of the whole ministry vision that God's given to you. And just as God is leading/guiding and blessing in other areas of the ministry, He's going to lead/guide and bless in the financial area of the ministry.

My suggestion to new ministry leaders is to start with their closest circle of supporters: immediate family members, close friends, and fellow church members. These individuals will likely be your lifelong core donors. They might not necessarily give extraordinarily large donations, but their donations are just as valuable, if not more valuable, than the larger donations you'll be receiving later. That's because these first donors, no matter how small their donations may be, are filled with the deepest trust and love you'll ever find. They join with you when you have nothing to show them. They have faith in you. And this is precious.

Next, I suggest a letter-writing campaign to persons in a wider social circle: extended family members, business acquaintances, potential donors, community leagues, and foundations dedicated to giving financial support to ministries and/or churches. Of course, contact with such persons/organizations doesn't have to be limited to letters. If you personally meet anyone in these categories, feel free to share with them your vision. You might even want to call several foundations to see if you can arrange a meeting with whomever is in charge of donations. One thing I discovered, much to my surprise, is that sometimes people don't need a lot of convincing. Many persons are eager to support a ministry, especially if a ministry leader is well-organized, articulate, and presents a vision with great passion and sincerity.

This brings up another important matter that relates directly to fundraising, as well as to securing ministry volunteers. You, as a leader, must remain authentic. A ministry leader must be honest and open about who they are. So, allow yourself to be vulnerable as you share your passion. Vulnerability has been called the forgotten virtue of leadership, especially these days when qualities like strength, savvy, training, and knowledge are more prized than anything else.

One way to keep yourself authentic and vulnerable is to be upfront not only about the strengths of your ministry, but also about its potential weaknesses. Be honest about what you can *really* accomplish and how far you can *really* go. Of course, being able to communicate your potential, and the potential of your ministry, requires a high degree of accurate self-assessment. And that is only possible through self-understanding, which is achieved only by way of emotional intelligence (see Chapter Five). Keeping it real, as the saying goes, will always result in respect (perhaps not always a donation, but always respect).

Authenticity will also help you during the tough times. You will not be wasting precious energy on keeping up a brave front if you're feeling drained. And fundraising can indeed be draining, especially in the early days of a ministry when it's more difficult to find donors. Just try to remember that people tend to support established ministries. Newer ministries have no track record. They're risky. And the leaders involved are unknown leaders with unknown qualities. For donors, it's almost like picking a stock in the stock market. There are the well-known and relatively safe corporations such as Apple, Facebook, Amazon, Disney, and Google. Then you have the unknown upstarts: Snap Inc.; Blue Apron; Interactive Intelligence Group; Ancestry.com. Which company would you feel most comfortable putting your money into as an investment?

Another large part of raising funds that few people ever think about involves simply finding the right name for a ministry. It's so important—the branding, the marketing, the notoriety. The right name, as opposed to the wrong name, can truly make a difference when it comes to getting donors to make a contribution. This might sound terribly carnal and worldly, but it's a reality. Michael Hyatt, former CEO of Thomas Nelson Publisher, said it perfectly through the title of his book, *Platform: Get Noticed in a Noisy World*. That is the challenge: getting noticed. One book that I'd recommend is *Effective Fundraising for Non-Profits: Real-World Strategies That Work*. This 474-page volume is packed with valuable information that every ministry leader should have at their fingertips. It has helped me and many others.

Finally, I always tell new ministry leaders that when it comes to raising funds, just spread the word about your ministry in as many ways as possible. Post your Vision/Mission Statement and contact information on bulletin boards all over the city. Join community groups, where you can meet potential donors and tell them about your ministry. Print brochures and/or flyers to leave on car windshields. Create business cards to hand out when you meet people at parties, church gatherings, or other social functions. Talk. Talk. Talk.

## GO FORWARD AND ONWARD

Well, here you are. You've arrived at the end of the book. I've shared with you everything God has led me to share. Now you have a choice to make—a choice that comes after all you've read, all you've thought, and all you've learned. I've given you the knowledge, the skills, and the encouragement to do something great for God. But will you? Are you going to put what you now know into practice? Do you want to make a difference?

Everything in this book will either become just head-knowledge to you that will be neatly tucked away in some dusty chamber of your mind, or everything you've learned will serve as a foundation on which you'll build a life-long legacy to the work of Christ in the world. I hope and pray you'll use all that I've shared with you to formulate a tangible plan that will lead you to supporting a ministry, then joining a ministry, and finally, starting a ministry.

I also pray your ministry becomes a thousand times more successful than any ministry now existing, including my own! You, as a NextGen leader, are the future of the Church. The health of God's Kingdom sits on *your* shoulders. The hope of the hopeless rests in your hands. "[H]ow can they call on him to save them unless they believe in him? And how can they believe in him if they have never heard about him? And how can they hear about him unless someone tells them? And how will anyone go and tell them without being sent? That is why the Scriptures say, 'How beautiful are the feet of messengers who bring good news!'" (Rom. 10:14–15).

I know this might sound like a heavy burden, but with God leading you, guiding you, strengthening you, energizing you, and fighting for you, "'everything is possible'" (Matt. 19:26). Then, when trials/tribulations come your way (and believe me, they'll come), just remember that you can still make a difference. The world will be watching. And they will see the example you set in the face of adversity (perhaps even failure). They'll learn from you; you'll help them endure. How is that possible? Because people get inspired when they see someone fighting for a cause, when they see someone not quitting, when they see someone showing courage. Remember, a vision remains alive not because of the vision itself, but because of the vision-bearer.

So, to every NextGen leader: *be persistent and persevering; be consistent and committed.* The fruit you bear will be more than you could ever ask for, think, or imagine (Eph. 3:20). Let the world see that your vision is truly alive in your heart. Display by your words and your deeds the beauty and wonder of what you want to accomplish for God. This is far more important than anything technical. As the famous French poet, Antoine de Saint-Exupéry (1900–1944), said, "If you want to build a ship, don't drum up people to collect wood and don't assign them tasks and work, but rather teach them to long for the endless immensity of the sea."

In conclusion, I want to share a word of both caution and encouragement. I've known many brothers and sisters who have become inspired by a book, church message, TV program, video, or crusade. And in response they've expressed a true desire to get involved. This is wonderful. Unfortunately, many of them haven't acted immediately on that inspiration. They've waited, putting their plans to participate in ministry on hold until: a) life becomes calmer; b) finances get better; c) time is more free; d) work isn't as hectic . . . etc. etc. etc. In other words, ministry involvement will happen for them when everything is in perfect order.

The truth, however, is that everything will *never* be in perfect order. Waiting for that never-to-be time will only keep you from *ever* supporting, joining, or starting a ministry. This is a favorite tactic used by the forces of darkness to keep us from God's work. If the Enemy can get us to just delay our plans long enough, then in all likelihood, our plans will never come to pass.

The most destructive things are often the small things that we're not guarding ourselves against. A big tragedy isn't needed. A huge roadblock of some kind is unnecessary. Minor end-on-end delays will do the trick. Eventually, nothing happens. And the Enemy wins. But instead of allowing Satan to have victory, you can join the ranks of those faithful men and women who have fought before you in the struggle for souls. Such individuals have been heroes of the faith, especially the ones who have braved many perils in the Middle East.

Consider the accomplishments of Lillian Trasher (b. 1887), for instance, who tirelessly worked among Egypt's orphans and other cast-offs from 1911, until her death in 1961. She founded the very first orphanage in Egypt and by the end of her life had cared for approximately 10,000 orphans. Not surprisingly, she was nicknamed "Mother" Thrasher.[154]

There was also Maurice Gerges (d. 2016), who toiled as an evangelist to the Arabic-speaking world for sixty years! Thousands came to Christ through his efforts, which moved many people to call him "the Billy Graham of the Middle East."[155]

And no one will forget Roy Whitman (d. 1992) and his wife, Dora (d. 1994), who moved to Jordan, where they served selflessly, until the end of their lives. They "lived a very frugal life. Most of the money that they received from supporters they gave away to others. They had a love for refugees, the poor, the blind, and the Bedouin. But most of all they wanted people to know Jesus."[156]

The time is *now*. If you want to support, join, or start a ministry, then the time is now. Life is short. Our days are fragile and limited, said Job, and can't be extended (Job 14:5). None of us knows how much time we have on this earth. But one thing we do know is that the years pass quickly. In fact, the older one gets, the more quickly the years seem to pass. So, if you feel the Lord tugging at your heart, even the least bit, I want to encourage you to make a commitment today—*right now*. As you're reading, just pray to the Lord, in the quietness of your heart:

*Yes, Lord God. I commit to you this day to either support, join, or start a ministry. I give to you all of my time, talent, and treasure to use as you see fit for your glory, for your kingdom, and for your people. Take my life in your hands and mold it into whatever you want it to be. Take me wherever you want me to go. Fill me with your power and your presence in a way I've never before known so that I can reach the lost for Christ. Enable me to do more than I ever thought possible. Show me the way to go. Destroy any fear I may have within my heart, and replace it with your courage to face all obstacles. Light a fire within that will burn so bright the whole world will see it—for your honor, your glory, and your purpose. Bring to me brothers and sisters with whom I can work to spread the good news of the gospel of Jesus Christ. And may the course of history and the future path of the globe somehow be changed through me.*

*In Jesus' mighty name, Amen!*

# ACKNOWLEDGMENTS

I could not have produced this book had it not been for the constant and unconditional love of my family. They, like so many others, have believed in me, encouraged me, and inspired me since the very beginning of my journey. I must first thank Aladdin and Kholoud Alayateem, who received me into their family when I first came to America. Additional thanks goes to Jadd and Jane Boulos, who encouraged and counseled me from the earliest days of my Christian faith. I'm also indebted to: Brian Satterlee, for preparing me for real-life while I was still a young man at college; Jacob Kakish, for giving me a chance to teach the Word of God; and Esper Ajaj, for inspiring me through his humility and perseverance. I'm equally grateful to: Dale O'Shields, for believing in me and supporting my ministry dreams; Nizar Shaheen, for his friendship and godly wisdom; Chip Ingram, for mentoring and coaching me; and Tony Nijmeh, for being a great advisor and a true friend. I also need to mention Richard Abanes, for the extensive research and editing skills he contributed to this book. And finally, a very special word of acknowledgment belongs to my NEXTGEN Dream Team, for their countless volunteering hours and dedication to the work of God around the world. I pray that our Lord will bless each and every one of you as we join together in serving our Savior, Jesus Christ, through the glorious work of the Kingdom.

# NOTES

## INTRODUCTION

[1] Simon Sinek, quoted in Graham Gorrel, "Graham Gorrel's Friday On My Mind," Nov. 18, 2016, The Daily Advertiser, http://www.dailyadvertiser.com.au/story/4298974/what-is-this-thing-called-leadership/.

[2] Rick Warren, The Purpose-Driven Life (Grand Rapids, MI: Zondervan, 2002; 2006 ed.), p. 17.

## CHAPTER 1

[3] Mark Batterson, interview with Christianity Today, "A City Upon 'The Hill,'" Christianity Today: CT Pastors, Summer 2008, http://www.christianitytoday.com/pastors/2008/summer/15.44.html.

[4] Aubrey Sequeira, "Re-Thinking Homogeneity: The Biblical Case for Multi-Ethnic Churches," 9Marks Journal, Sept. 25, 2015, https://9marks.org/article/re-thinking-homogeneity-the-biblical-case-for-multi-ethnic-churches/.

[5] Sequeira, https://9marks.org/article/re-thinking-homogeneity-the-biblical-case-for-multi-ethnic-churches/.

[6] John S. Dickerson, interview with Trevin Wax, "The Great Evangelical Recession? A Conversation with John Dickerson," Jan. 10, 2013, https://blogs.thegospelcoalition.org/trevinwax/2013/01/10/the-great-evangelical-recession-a-conversation-with-john-dickerson/.

[7] Bob Smietana, "The Changing Face of the American Church," Facts & Trends, Oct. 2, 2014.

[8] Bob Smietana, "Sunday Morning Segregation: Most Worshipers Feel Their Church Has Enough Diversity," Christianity Today, Jan. 2015, http://www.christianitytoday.com/gleanings/2015/january/sunday-morning-segregation-most-worshipers-church-diversity.html.

[9] Ed Stetzer, quoted in Smietana, "Sunday Morning," http://www.christianitytoday.com/gleanings/2015/january/sunday-morning-segregation-most-worshipers-church-diversity.html.

[10] Mark DeYmaz, quoted in "The Theology of Multi-Ethnic Church," Christianity Today, June 2010, http://www.christianitytoday.com/pastors/2010/june-online-only/theology-of-multi-ethnic-church.html.

[11] Mark DeYmaz, "Mono-Ethnic Ministries and Multi-Ethnic Churches (Part 1)," Christianity Today, Aug. 2010, http://www.christianitytoday.com/pastors/2010/june-online-only/theology-of-multi-ethnic-church.html.

[12] Bill Hybels, Courageous Leadership (Grand Rapids, MI: Zondervan, 2002; 2009 ed.), p. 23.

[13] Mark D. Roberts, "What Is A Church," Reflections on Christ, Church, and Culture Blog, online at Patheos, http://www.patheos.com/blogs/markdroberts/series/what-is-a-church/.

[14] Albert Barnes, Barnes's Notes On the New Bible, http://biblehub.com/commentaries/ephesians/1-23.htm.

[15] Barnes, http://biblehub.com/commentaries/ephesians/1-23.htm.

[16] Dr. Charlie Bing, "Characteristics of a Grace-oriented Church," Grace Life, online edition, http://www.gracelife.org/resources/gracenotes/?id=4.

[17] Charles Spurgeon, The Complete Works of C. H. Spurgeon, Volume 14: Sermons 788 to 847 (Harrington, DE: Delmarva Publications, 2013), "Sermon #806: A Young Man's Vision," Apr. 6, 1868.

## CHAPTER 2

[18] Dale O'Shields, Living & Giving God's Dream (Gaithersburg, MD; Practical Living Press, 2017) pp. 7.

[19] Louie Giglio, The Comeback: It's Not Too Late and You're Never too Far (Nashville, TN: W Publishing Group, 2015), p. 47.

[20] Craig Groeschel, 2015 Network Summit, quoted in Lifeway Leadership, "Best Quotes From Life Church Network Summit," Lifeway Leadership Website, Oct. 26, 2915, http://www.lifeway.com/leadership/2015/10/26/best-quotes-from-life-church-network-summit/.

[21] Craig Groeschel, How Churches and Leaders Can Get it and Keep It (Grand Rapids, MI: Zondervan, 2008), p. 98

[22] A21, "Our Mission," http://www.a21.org/content/who-we-are/gnihwo.

[23] Christine Cain, "Perspective of Purpose," http://christinecaine.com/content/perspective-of-purpose/gjenlq?permcode=gjenlq&site=true.

[24] Maher Samuel, "ISIS and Christ: Culture of Death and Culture of Life," sermon first

broadcast live from Kasr El Dobara Evangelical Church, Cairo, Egypt, Nov. 2014, https://www.youtube.com/watch?v=OKUZlglTyYw.

## CHAPTER 3

[25] Hollie Shaw,"Glocalization Rules the World," Financial Times, May 20, 2011, http://business.financialpost.com/news/glocalization-rules-the-world.

[26] Victor Roudometof, Glocalization: A Critical Introduction (New York, NY: Routledge, 2016), p. 2.

[27] U.S. News & World Report, Dec. 31, 1990 - Jan. 7, 1991, p. 84, quoted in Toshie M. Evans, A Dictionary of Japanese Loan Words (Westport, CT: Greenwood Press, 1997), p. 42.

[28] Roudometof, p. 3.

[29] Roudometof, p. 3.

[30] Roland Robertson, "The Conceptual Promise of Glocalization: Commonality and Diversity," Art-e-Fact, Issue #4, Dec. 2005, http://artefact.mi2.hr/_a04/lang_en/theory_robertson_en.htm.

[31] Bob Roberts, Jr., Glocalization: How Followers of Jesus Engage a Flat World (Grand Rapids, MI: Zondervan, 2007), p. 14.

[32] "Without Shackles, no date, see Al Hayat Ministries at http://alhayat.org/en-us/ourprograms/withoutshackles.aspx for more information.

[33] Edwin M. Yamauchi, "On the Road With Paul," Christian History, http://www.christianitytoday.com/history/issues/issue-47/on-road-with-paul.html.

[34] "Early Christians," PBS, http://www.pbs.org/empires/romans/empire/christians.html.

[35] "The Spread of Christianity," Jewish History, http://www.jewishhistory.org/the-spread-of-christianity/.

[36] see Rick Warren, "3 Phases of a Paul and Timothy Relationship," http://pastors.com/paul-timothy/.

[37] Warren, http://pastors.com/paul-timothy/.

[38] Mark Ballenger, "How to Find a Christian Mentor," http://applygodsword.com/how-to-find-a-christian-mentor/.

[39] Daniel Fusco, "A Snapshot of our Paul, Barnabas and Timothy Model of Mentoring," Oct. 24, 2011, http://www.danielfusco.com/blog/a-snapshot-of-our-paul-barnabas-and-timothy-model-of-mentoring/.

[40] The "A" in Dolan's originally article stood for "ASSIGNABLE," meaning to make sure to

assign specific duties, to specific persons, for specific reasons.

[41] Queen Rania Al-Abdullah, quoted in "What Queen Rania wants for the world," excerpts from The Oprah Winfrey Show, CNN, July 14, 2008, http://edition.cnn.com/2008/LIVING/wayoflife/07/14/o.women.changing.world/index.html.

## CHAPTER 4

[42] Chip Ingram, The Real God (Grand Rapids, MI; Baker Books, 2016) pp. 33.

[43] Chip Ingram, True Spirituality (New York, NY; Howard Books, 2009), pp. 1, 48, 103, 167, 227.

[44] Chip Ingram, interview with Susie Larson, Live the Promise, 2014, http://myfaithradio.com/2014/true-spirituality/.

[45] Christine Cain, "Perspective of Purpose," http://christinecaine.com/content/perspective-of-purpose/gjenlq?permcode=gjenlq&site=true.

[46] Christopher Abel, "What Does the "Living" Word Really Mean?," Relevant, Oct. 1, 2012, http://archives.relevantmagazine.com/god/practical-faith/what-does-living-word-really-mean.

[47] "Mueller's Time In Devon," https://www.mullers.org/find-out-more-1829.

[48] Arthur Tappan Pierson, George Müller of Bristol (London: James Nisbet & Co., Limited, 1899), pp. 407-408.

[49] George Mueller, quoted in Roy B. Zuck, The Speaker's Quote Book: Over 5,000 Illustrations and Quotations (Grand Rapids, MI: Kregel Publications, 1997; 2009 rev. ed.), p. 185.

[50] George Mueller, The Autobiography of George Mueller (New Kensington, PA: Whitaker House, 1984) pp. 155-156.

[51] George Mueller, quoted in Martin H. Manser, The Westminster Collection of Christian Quotations (Louisville, KY: Westminster John Knox Press, 2001), p. 287.

[52] Matt Tully, "What George Mueller Can Teach Us about Prayer," online article adapted from Donald S. Whitney, Praying the Bible (Wheaton, IL: Crossway Books, 2015), https://www.crossway.org/blog/2015/07/what-george-mueller-can-teach-us-about-prayer/.

[53] Hank Hannegraaff, "Thanksgiving and the F-A-C-T-S on Prayer," online article, http://www.equip.org/article/thanksgiving-f-c-t-s-prayer/.

[54] Mark Batterson, quoted in Michael Duduit, "Praying and Preaching: An Interview with Mark Batterson," Preaching, https://www.preaching.com/articles/praying-and-preaching-an-interview-with-mark-batterson/.

55 Phil Briggs, "Prayer: Your power connection," Lifeway Devotional, http://www.lifeway.com/Article/Parenting-teens-family-Prayer-your-power-connection.

56 R.A. Torrey, How to Pray, Chapter X, online edition, http://www.ccel.org/ccel/torrey/pray.i_1.xiii.html.

57 Bill Hybels, Just Walk Across the Room: Simple Steps Pointing People to Faith (Grand Rapids, MI: Zondervan, 2006), p. 204.

58 Max Lucado, Before Amen: The Power of a Simple Prayer (Nashville, TN: Thomas Nelson), p. 9.

59 Max Lucado, interview with Jonathan Peterson, Bible Gateway Blog, Oct. 6, 2014, https://www.biblegateway.com/blog/2014/10/what-to-say-before-amen-an-interview-with-max-lucado/.

60 Lucado, Before Amen, p. 1.

61 Dr. Ghassan Khalaf, "Meanings of Pentecost," message delivered at Arabic Calvary Chapel, no date, https://www.youtube.com/watch?v=7aotDgZqKBY&index=14&list=PLnSDPWb57wtkW-CCVd0CJU9amn4zR4wWS.

62 SAT-7, "Christian Television by and for the People of the Middle East and North Africa," https://www.sat7uk.org/#February-2015. This television show—affiliated with one of our own ministry partners SAT-7—is based in the Middle East and broadcasts in Arabic, Turkish and Farsi to 500 million people. It seeks to "make the Gospel, the local church, and rights and freedoms visible. . . . [And] is committed to holistic programming, with the aim of ministering to people in all areas of their life: spiritual, emotional, psychological and physical."

63 SAT-7, Interview with Myriam, Sat-7 TV, https://www.youtube.com/watch?v=_ige6CcXuMg.

## CHAPTER 5

64 "Emotional Intelligence," Psychology Today, Glossary, https://www.psychologytoday.com/basics/emotional-intelligence.

65 Online Oxford Dictionary, https://en.oxforddictionaries.com/definition/intelligence_quotient.

66 Susan Krauss Whitbourne, "Unlock Your Emotional Genius," Psychology Today, Feb. 2, 2013, https://www.psychologytoday.com/blog/fulfillment-any-age/201302/unlock-your-emotional-genius.

67 Graham Jones, paraphrased/cited by Whitbourne, https://www.psychologytoday.com/blog/fulfillment-any-age/201302/unlock-your-emotional-genius.

[68] John D. Mayer, "What Emotional Intelligence Is and Is Not," Psychology Today, Sept. 21, 2009, https://www.psychologytoday.com/blog/the-personality-analyst/200909/what-emotional-intelligence-is-and-is-not. This is Part One of an article that originally appeared in Charaktery Magazine, a Polish-language publication.

[69] Darbie Saxbe, "The Socially Savvy," Psychology Today, Nov. 1, 2004, https://www.psychologytoday.com/articles/200411/the-socially-savvy.

[70] Talent Smart, "About Emotional Intelligence," http://www.talentsmart.com/about/emotional-intelligence.php.

[71] Jose M. Mestre and Kimberly A Barchard, "4 signs you have high emotional intelligence, according to academic experts," Business Insider, Apr. 16, 2017, http://www.businessinsider.com/4-signs-you-have-high-emotional-intelligence-according-to-academic-experts-2017-4.

[72] Adam Toren, "Are You Emotionally Intelligent? It'll Help You Rise Above Failure." NBC News, Feb. 27, 2014, http://www.nbcnews.com/id/54531766/ns/business-small_business/t/are-you-emotionally-intelligent-itll-help-you-rise-above-failure/#.WPe2xBiZN24.

[73] Mestre and Barchard, http://www.businessinsider.com/4-signs-you-have-high-emotional-intelligence-according-to-academic-experts-2017-4.

[74] Talent Smart, "About Emotional Intelligence," http://www.talentsmart.com/about/emotional-intelligence.php.

[75] John Piper, "Pastor, Know Thyself," Christianity Today, Feb. 2013, http://www.christianitytoday.com/pastors/2013/february-online-only/pastor-know-thyself.html.

[76] Daniel Coleman, quoted in Elizabeth Treher, David Piltz, Steven Jacobs, A Guide to Success for Technical Managers (Hoboken, NJ: Wiley & Sons, 2011), p. 283.

[77] John C. Maxwell, How Successful People Lead (New York, NY: Center Street, 2013), p. 6.

[78] Travis Bradberry, "Emotional Intelligence—EQ," Forbes, Jan. 9, 2014, https://www.forbes.com/sites/travisbradberry/2014/01/09/emotional-intelligence/#63119fa21ac0.

[79] Mestre and Barchard, http://www.businessinsider.com/4-signs-you-have-high-emotional-intelligence-according-to-academic-experts-2017-4.

## CHAPTER 6

[80] Richard Stearns, The Hole in Our Gospel (Nashville, TN: Thomas Nelson, 2009), p. 259.

[81] Francis Chan, "New Thoughts: Something God Taught Me," Jan. 28, 2008, https://www.youtube.com/watch?v=XKzYQMbQKSw.

[82] Edward F. Markquart, "Series A — Talents: Five, Two, and One," Sermons From Seattle, http://www.sermonsfromseattle.com/series_a_talents.htm.

[83] John C. Maxwell, Sometimes You Win, Sometimes You Learn (New York, NY: Center Street, 2013), p. 16.

[84] Rick Warren, "Make The Most Of Your Talents," May 21, 2014, http://pastorrick.com/devotional/english/make-the-most-of-your-talents.

[85] see C.S. Lewis, A Grief Observed (New York, NY: Harper Collins, 1994); Corrie Ten Boom, The Hiding Place (Grand Rapids, MI: Chosen Books, 2006); and Joni Eareckson Tada, Joni (Grand Rapids, MI: Zondervan, 2001).

[86] Chris Hodges, "The CE Interview: Chris Hodges," Church Executive, Nov. 15, 2015, https://churchexecutive.com/archives/the-ce-interview-4.

[87] A.J. Baime, "How Detroit Won World War II," 12/5/14, http://www.scout.com/military/warrior/story/1488540-how-detroit-won-world-war-ii; cf. A.J. Baime, The Arsenal of Democracy (New York, NY: Houghton, Mifflin, Harcourt, 2014).

[88] Baime, http://www.scout.com/military/warrior/story/1488540-how-detroit-won-world-war-ii.

[89] Baime, http://www.scout.com/military/warrior/story/1488540-how-detroit-won-world-war-ii.

[90] Baime, http://www.scout.com/military/warrior/story/1488540-how-detroit-won-world-war-ii.

[91] Charles Sorenson, "Production Miracle At Willow Run," Strategos, Sept. 2007, http://www.strategosinc.com/willow_run.htm; excerpted from Charles Sorenson, My Forty Years With Ford (Detroit, MI: Wayne State University Press, 2006).

[92] Nizar Shaheen, interview with David Maines, 2003, https://www.youtube.com/watch?v=WP9zXUmZuVY.

[93] Light For All Nations, https://www.lfan.org/our-ministry/about.

[94] Light For All Nations, https://www.lfan.org/our-ministry/about.

[95] Light For All Nations, https://www.lfan.org/our-ministry/ministry-activities.

[96] Nizar Shareef, Light For All Nations, May 2017 Newsletter.

[97] Shareef, Light For All Nations, May 2017 Newsletter.

[98] Nizar Shareef, Light For All Nations, June 2017 Newsletter.

## CHAPTER 7

[99] Ravi Zacharias, interview with Baltimore Post-Examiner, "Ravi Zacharias: Christian apologist proclaims a reasonable faith," Baltimore Post-Examiner, May 24, 2015, http://

baltimorepostexaminer.com/ravi-zacharias-christian-apologist-proclaims-a-reasonable-faith/2015/05/24#sthash.dMqu48Lq.dpuf:.

[100] Brittney Dawney and Joshua M. Pearce, "Optimizing the solar water disinfection (SODIS) method by decreasing turbidity with NaCl," Journal of Water, Sanitation and Hygiene for Development 2(2) pp., 87-94 (2012), http://www.academia.edu/1529175/Optimizing_the_solar_water_disinfection_SODIS_method_by_decreasing_turbidity_with_NaCl.

[101] Michael B. Kelley, "This Guy Is Making Dirty Water Safe To Drink By Using A Common Kitchen Ingredient," Business Insider, May 8, 2012, http://www.businessinsider.com/clean-drinking-water-using-table-salt-2012-5.

[102] Adrian Burton, "Purifying Drinking Water with Sun, Salt, and Limes," Environ Health Perspect 8/2012; 120(8): a305, https://www.ncbi.nlm.nih.gov/pmc/articles/PMC3440092/.

[103] Kelley, http://www.businessinsider.com/clean-drinking-water-using-table-salt-2012-5.

[104] T.V. Philip, "Salt and Light (Matthew 5:13-16)," http://www.religion-online.org/showarticle.asp?title=1528.

[105] John Stott, "John Stott: Four Ways Christians Can Influence the World," Christianity Today, Oct. 20, 2011, http://www.christianitytoday.com/ct/2011/october/saltlight.html?start=2.

[106] Kara Fox and Dave Gilbert, "Terror attacks in developed world surge 650% in one year," CNN, Nov. 16, 2016, http://www.cnn.com/2016/11/16/world/global-terrorism-report/.

[107] Fox and Gilbert, http://www.cnn.com/2016/11/16/world/global-terrorism-report/.

[108] "SYRIA: Islamic State Executes Three Christians," Canada Free Press, Oct. 15, 2015, http://canadafreepress.com/article/syria-islamic-state-executes-three-christians.

[109] World Health Organization, "Executive Summary," http://www.who.int/whr/1995/media_centre/executive_summary1/en/.

[110] World Health Organization, http://www.who.int/whr/1995/media_centre/executive_summary1/en/.

[111] The Hunger Project, "Know Your World: Facts About Hunger and Poverty," http://www.thp.org/knowledge-center/know-your-world-facts-about-hunger-poverty/.

[112] John Clarke, "Nuclear 'Doomsday Clock' ticks closest to midnight in 64 years," Bulletin of the Atomic Scientists, Jan. 2017, http://www.reuters.com/article/us-science-doomsdayclock-idUSKBN15A2JJ.

[113] John Mecklin, ed. and Science and Security Board, Bulletin of the Atomic Scientists, "It is two and a half minutes to midnight," Bulletin of the Atomic Scientists, http://thebulletin.org/sites/default/files/Final%202017%20Clock%20Statement.pdf.

[114] Anup Shah, "Climate Change and Global Warming," Global Issues, Feb. 2, 2015, http://www.globalissues.org/issue/178/climate-change-and-global-warming.

[115] Bethenny Watters, "How Do Trees Turn Carbon Dioxide Into Oxygen?," Sciencing, Apr. 25, 2017, http://sciencing.com/trees-turn-carbon-dioxide-oxygen-10034022.html.

[116] Nils Zimmermann, "Five of the world's biggest environmental problems," DW, Oct. 11, 2016, http://www.dw.com/en/five-of-the-worlds-biggest-environmental-problems/a-35915705.

[117] AC Shilton, "What Would Happen if All the Bees Died Tomorrow?," Tonic, Mar. 1, 2017, https://tonic.vice.com/en_us/article/what-would-happen-if-all-the-bees-died-tomorrow.

[118] All quotes cited in Anne Marie Helmenstine, Ph.D., "How Much Oxygen Does One Tree Produce?," ThoughtCo., Apr. 10, 2017, https://www.thoughtco.com/how-much-oxygen-does-one-tree-produce-606785.

[119] Jack Hall, "The Most Important Organism, Ecology: Earth, Sept. 12, 2011, http://www.ecology.com/2011/09/12/important-organism/.

[120] Zimmermann, http://www.dw.com/en/five-of-the-worlds-biggest-environmental-problems/a-35915705.

[121] World Wildlife Fund, "Soil Erosion and Degredation," https://www.worldwildlife.org/threats/soil-erosion-and-degradation.

[122] John Piper, "You Shall Receive Power...For Mission," Desiring God, Oct. 16, 1988, http://www.desiringgod.org/messages/you-shall-receive-powerfor-mission.

[123] Piper, http://www.desiringgod.org/messages/you-shall-receive-powerfor-mission.

[124] Piper, http://www.desiringgod.org/messages/you-shall-receive-powerfor-mission.

[125] Piper, http://www.desiringgod.org/messages/you-shall-receive-powerfor-mission.

[126] Piper, http://www.desiringgod.org/messages/you-shall-receive-powerfor-mission.

[127] Finishing the Task Report, "What is the Task," http://www.finishingthetask.com.

[128] Finishing the Task Report, "The UUPG List," http://www.finishingthetask.com/uupgs.php?sort=Country.

[129] Finishing the Task Report, "Finishing the Task Progress," http://www.finishingthetask.com/stats.htm. 96 have no written scriptures; 1,668 have no oral scriptures; 1,256 have no Jesus Film; 2,484 have no faith/evangelistic film; 2,071 have no radio broadcast available; 666 have no gospel recordings.

[130] Paul Eshleman, "Letter from the Director," Finishing the Task Workbook, Dec. 16, 2016-Dec. 8, 2016 Conference, introduction.

[131] Finishing the Task Workbook, p. 15.

[132] Justin J. Evans (Research Assistant, Center for the Study of Global Christianity, Gordon-Conwell University), email from Gordon-Conwell Theological Seminary, "Global Christianity," to Ms. Shenandoah Brown, SFO (Secular Franciscan Order), quoted in "The Facts and Stats on '33,000 Denominations,'" http://www.biblicalcatholic.com/apologetics/a106.htm; cf. ThoughtCo, "Christianity Statistics," https://www.thoughtco.com/christianity-statistics-700533.

[133] Mary Fairchild, "Christianity Statistics," ThoughtCo, Mar. 14, 2017, https://www.thoughtco.com/christianity-statistics-700533.

[134] Fairchild, https://www.thoughtco.com/christianity-statistics-700533.

[135] Joshua Project, "Has Everyone Heard," https://joshuaproject.net/resources/articles/has_everyone_heard.

[136] Issachar Initiative, "About the Issachar Initiative," http://issacharinitiative.org/about/.

## CHAPTER 8

[137] Joel C. Hunter, Church Distributed (Longwood, FL: Distributed Church Press, 2007), p. 47

[138] Hospitality Homes, "Welcome," http://www.hospitalityhomes.org.

[139] New Life, "Ways to Give," http://newlife.com/why-give/.

[140] Chris Hodges, "The CE Interview: Chris Hodges," Church Executive, Nov. 15, 2015, https://churchexecutive.com/archives/the-ce-interview-4.

[141] R.A. Torrey, The Power of Prayer and the Prayer of Power (New York, NY: Cosimo Classics, 2009), p. 17.

[142] "Preparing to Enter the Land (Joshua 2:1-24)," Studies in the Life of Joshua, https://bible.org/seriespage/2-preparing-enter-land-joshua-21-24.

[143] Shaun Spearmon, "Your Company Vision: If It's Complicated, It Shouldn't Be," Forbes, Oct. 14, 2013, https://www.forbes.com/sites/johnkotter/2013/10/14/the-reason-most-company-vision-statements-arent-effective/#728d4fe22dc7.

[144] Spearmon, https://www.forbes.com/sites/johnkotter/2013/10/14/the-reason-most-company-vision-statements-arent-effective/#728d4fe22dc7.

[145] Tom Wright, "How to Write a Good Vision Statement," Dec. 10, 2014, https://www.executestrategy.net/blog/write-good-vision-statement/.

[146] Spearmon, https://www.forbes.com/sites/johnkotter/2013/10/14/the-reason-most-company-vision-statements-arent-effective/#728d4fe22dc7.

147 Community Tool Box, http://ctb.ku.edu/en/table-of-contents/structure/strategic-planning/vision-mission-statements/main.

148 Community Tool Box, http://ctb.ku.edu/en/table-of-contents/structure/strategic-planning/vision-mission-statements/main.

149 Community Tool Box, http://ctb.ku.edu/en/table-of-contents/structure/strategic-planning/vision-mission-statements/main.

150 Bob Thune, "Strategic Planning for Ministry: How to Write a Mission Statement," Dec. 31, 2013, http://www.bobthune.com/2013/12/strategic-planning-for-ministry-how-to-write-a-mission-statement/.

151 Ministry Venture, "An Effective Vision and Mission Statement for Your Ministry," https://ministryventures.org/an-effective-vision-and-mission-statement-for-your-ministry.

152 Craig Groeschel, It: How Churches and Leaders Can Get It and Keep It (Grand Rapids, MI: Zondervan, 2011), p. 48.

153 Rick Warren, "Three Benefits of Telling Others About Your Dream," Pastor Rick's Daily Hope, Apr. 29, 2015, http://pastorrick.com/devotional/english/full-post/three-benefits-of-telling-others-about-your-dream.

154 "Lillian trasher Biography," http://www.inspirationalchristians.org/biography/lillian-trasher/.

155 Bader Mansour, "Maurice Gerges – the Famous Preacher You have Never Heard Of - By Bader Mansour," Come and See, Apr. 14, 2016, http://www.comeandsee.com/view.php?sid=1310.

156 Roy and Dora Whitman Academy, "History of Roy and Dora," http://whitmanacademy.org/general-info/quarter-4.

# LEV/\NT
## MINISTRIES

### We **SHARE**
the Good News of Jesus with all
Arabic-speaking people

### We **EQUIP**
believers with essential
spiritual resources

### We **MOBILIZE**
the next generation of leaders

## The Levant Region
Today, the Levant consists of Lebanon,
Syria, Jordan, Palestine, Israel, Egypt, and
Iraq. The Levant has been described as the
"crossroads" of western Asia, the eastern
Mediterranean and northeast Africa.

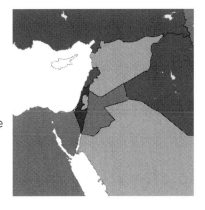

Learn more about Levant by visiting
## LEVANTMINISTRIES.ORG

# NE✕TGEN
## LEADERS INITIATIVE

**PURPOSE**

This initiative was created to fulfill the mandate of 2 Timothy 2:2:

> "The things which you have heard from me in the presence of many witnesses, entrust these to faithful men." (NASB)

**MISSION**

Our mission is to connect leaders together, equip them with resources, and send them to change communities.

**VISION**

Our vision is to be the generation who lives out the faith to transform the world by the love and hope of Jesus Christ.

## ABOUT NEXTGEN

NEXTGEN was created to meet the felt need that existed within the church for a plan that was focused on raising the next generation of leaders. NEXTGEN was able to meet that demand by developing a program specifically focused on millennials (ages 18-35). With a unique approach to programming and learning, this initiative will help young leaders fulfill their God-given dreams, encourage pastors and church leaders, and support the church to lean toward the next generation.

## PROGRAMS

We connect, equip, and mobilize the next generation of leaders through the following programs:

AN INITIATIVE OF
L E V∧N T
M I N I S T R I E S

*Learn More at nextgenlead.org*